Becoming Spiritual

A Prelude to the Apostolic for God's People

Calvin B. Collins, Sr.

Kingdom Journey Press
A Division of Kingdom Journey Enterprises
Woodbridge, VA

Copyright Instructions
Becoming Spiritual: A Prelude to the Apostolic for God's People
Copyright 2014 by Calvin B. Collins, Sr.

Unless a person is explicitly identified by name, the statements that are used should not be directly attributed to any specific person.

All rights reserved under the international copyright law. No part of this book may be reproduced or transmitted in any form or by any means, electronic or mechanical, including photocopying, recording, or by any information storage and retrieval system, without the express, written permission of the author. The exception is reviewers, who may quote brief passages in a review.

Unless otherwise marked, all Scripture quotations are referenced from the King James Version of the Bible.

ISBN-10: 0989087808
ISBN-13: 978-0-9890878-0-3

Printed in the United States of America.

Published by Kingdom Journey Press
A Division of Kingdom Journey Enterprises, Woodbridge, VA
www.kjpressinc.com

Cover Design by Brand U Inc.

DEDICATION

To my wife Kimberly, who has always had a strong passion for Jesus Christ since the time we first met twenty-three years ago. Without you and your prayers for me, it's possible this day may have not come to past. By the grace of God, I have made it this far with you by my side working together. Your love and dedication have been with me since day one and I want to thank you for believing in me. What a great encourager you are, and wonderful wife and mother as well.

To my lovely children CJ, Karington and Karia, who have been with us since the beginning of the ministry as well. Thank you for many days of commitment and understanding for the work that we do. You continue to demonstrate love and kindness towards God, your parents and others, and I am extremely proud of that. I am proud to have such blessed children who understand their purpose in life as Christians.

To all of my spiritual sons and daughters of Healing and Restoration Discipleship Center (HRDC), who have graciously accepted the call of God to be a part of our first prophetic team of Christians and who understand their role and positions in the kingdom of God. It has been an honor to help transform, mentor, train and equip every one of you. I proudly salute the "A" team of our ministry. You are a part of history. You are playing a major role in helping to lay the foundation to provide the right atmosphere and morale for new Christian believers to experience. I am most humbled to have been selected by God to prepare such a great body of people as you. You have given me, my wife and family great inspiration to march forward into the apostolic and prophetic movement. Your humility, willingness and zeal for Jesus Christ played a major role in my writing this book. I am sure you will enjoy reading this book as well as many others because you were present word for word, moment by moment and deliverance after deliverance. I am Godly proud to see the fruits of my labor operating in you.

I dedicate this book to the "A" team!

Table of Contents

Foreword by Apostle Dennis R. Jacobs viii

Foreword by Apostle Sherylann Bragton ix

Foreword by Carol Ellis xii

Foreword by Pastor Tony Outlaw xiv

Preface xvi

Introduction xx

Chapter 1-The Purpose of the Holy Spirit 1

Chapter 2-The Spirit Reveals Things to Us 17

Chapter 3-Knowing What To Say in Hard Times 31

Chapter 4-The Danger Of Trusting In Ourselves 41

Chapter 5-Letting the Holy Spirit Lead You 53

Chapter 6-Things You Must Do 65

Chapter 7-Identifying Vital Signs 77

Chapter 8-Understanding Burdens 87

Chapter 9-Defeating the Spirit of Denial 97

Chapter 10-Defeating the Spirit of Fear 107

Chapter 11-Being Made Aware of the Times 121

About The Author..133

About Kingdom Journey Press 135

Foreword by Apostle Dennis R. Jacobs

This book reveals a well thought out approach for believers of any level to understand the basics of relationship with Christ and spiritual warfare. As I read through the pages I watched the progression of thoughts develop to a solid understanding on how to mature your spiritual life. Beginning with the purpose of the Holy Spirit and progressing to how the Holy Spirit reveals to us the world around us and in us and how to be led by Him.

The progression of thought brings you the defeat of entities that trouble and burden you. Things are concluded with an understanding of awareness of the times, which we all can use some insight into.

This book is recommended for all new believers to help gain a quick and concise understanding of their beginning walk with Christ. The older the believer who may only have the fundamentals of the kingdom will be enlightened, amazed and refreshed with the clear insight given by Apostle Collins.

Take this book and cherish it, love it, read and reread it, and digest this material. It will certainly be an enriching experience, buy an extra copy and share it with your friends. Have group discussions concerning the principles in it. You will certainly be benefitted by the good work contained within the pages. I recommend this book to all believers who are looking to gain a better understanding of the warfare in the spirit. The Grace of God be with you.

Apostle Dennis R. Jacobs
The Word Warehouse, Senior Pastor

Foreword by Apostle Sherylann Bragton

This book is GOD Sent! I believe that GOD especially downloaded this message into Pastor Calvin's spirit deliberately for this end time. As I read this book I discerned the message GOD is sending to the body of Christ.

> Body of CHRIST….. GET READY!
> THE TIME IS AT HAND!
> CALLING ALL SOLDIERS!
> CALLING ALL WARRIORS!
> THE CLARION CALL!
> SOUND THE SHOFAR!
> GOD Is Calling Us To Order!

God is calling together HIS army on one accord! Assembling HIS great army for this latter day, latter rain move of God. We are in a battle and in this battle there is no demilitarized zone! We Must Be <u>One Strong Healthy Body</u>, no longer being tossed to and fro by the enemy through our souls (lower nature). GOD is saying to the body of CHRIST, His people, His children, the Christians and Messianic Jews, "Go and Glean the Harvest! Go And Get My Lost, ALL Souls belong to ME!"

In order for us to carry out GOD'S orders, we must be solid ourselves! We must be separate from the world (satan), the spirit of the world; no longer Christians who are victims of it's snares. In this book, GOD reveals how the Christian can have Victory and Walk in Victory in his or her own personal life in the inward parts, the hidden places, the secret places that nobody sees, which is where the real struggle takes place!

Oh YES! It Really Is Possible to live the Highlife, the Victorious Life, the Abundant Life Right Here in the Earth, but it's ONLY through CHRIST JESUS by HIS SPIRIT, by Faith & by HIS WORD!

That's *Becoming Spiritual*!

Becoming Spiritual is abandoning this world or natural realm in order to be effective in carrying out the mission or mandate GOD given over our lives as vessels for Christ in this Earth, instead of being weighed down and trapped by the devil through our souls by sin, weaknesses and appetites that do not align with GOD and His Kingdom Authority. This state of being renders us powerless, impotent and stuck, being cheated of bearing fruit because we have become victims of our lower nature, unable to carry out our mission in life, our GOD Given mandate which results in many souls going to Hell or being bound while here on Earth because they were our assignment and we were not in place.

Not becoming spiritual is to have an identity crisis. To know who you are In CHRIST is to become naturally supernatural people because we are in this world but not from or of it. It should come naturally for us to operate out of the kingdom mindset, the Jesus mindset since we are citizens of heaven, but it must be developed in us (the mind of Christ) by the Holy Spirit, then we can dominate this world with the Love and the Power of JESUS CHRIST, our mentor, and change it to make it match the Kingdom of Heaven. Pastor Calvin does an excellent job, breaking down passionately the steps of conquering the soul by becoming spiritual people in order to finish complete that good work already finished by the Power of GOD within You!

As I read this book I found myself smiling and experiencing the JOY of the LORD because of the hope it's contents gave me in realizing there is hope for us ALL!

If you feel stuck today, I strongly recommend and encourage you to read this book! Follow as God, through Pastor Calvin, walks you step-by-step into Liberty and Victory from within to without in your everyday life as the head and not the tail! Above only and <u>Never</u> beneath, realizing that you are the righteousness of GOD, FULL of HIS Generous Benefits and Abundant Life! Your End Result Will Be *Becoming Spiritual*!

CONGRATULATIONS Pastor Calvin on this Beautiful book GOD has downloaded into you, and Blessed you to spill out into the Earth this life changing revelation to set the captives free!

I believe this book is one of GOD'S treasures in the Earth in these last days, A Spiritual Gold Mine to enrich the lives of the believer and to draw the weary soul to CHRIST, giving him and her Power For Living!!!

GOD BLESS You Man of GOD & My Very Dear Friend! Thank You for Your Integrity, Anointing and Your Example as well as Your Dedication and Determination to Feed and Equip HIS Lamb & to Be That Authority The LORD Has Placed You Here to Be!

Much Love and GOD'S Success to You as You Build GOD'S Kingdom in the Earth! My Prayers Are With You!

Apostle Sherylann Bragton
City of Love Ministries
Fredericksburg, VA

Foreword by Carol Ellis

By faith Abraham, when he was called, obeyed by going out to a place which he was to receive for an inheritance; and he went out, not knowing where he was going. Heb. 11:8

Several years ago I met a man who heard God call him "to go out" from the place that he had known as home for his heart, his faith, his ministry and I can tell you from listening to him that he did not know where he was going. He just knew he had heard the voice of God calling him to follow and to trust Him. Thus began a spiritual journey that would bring to light the kind intention of God's will for this man to become a father to many. This father to many is Calvin Collins.

I have witnessed firsthand the passion for truth and discipleship that both Calvin and Kim carry for the people of God. They are sojourning in a land of promise with its trials and difficulties that accompany every true word of God and they are dwelling in this land and cultivating faithfulness. Their love of God's people and the care for their well-being will be hallmark of their testimony passed on to the next generation of believers.

I Timothy 1:5 says, "But the goal of all instruction is love from a pure heart and a good conscience and a sincere faith." Galatians 5 also speaks to a bottom line of the gospel which is "faith working through love". Godly instruction from those who have been given the charge to teach, exhort, encourage, admonish and bring an 'administration suitable to the fullness of the times' carries a grave responsibility before God to present faith, love and instruction as a trinity of service to the hearts of His people. This takes time, patience, endurance and a strong desire to work from seed to harvest with the planting of the Lord in the lives of those served. Calvin and Kim are such laborers and caretakers over the people of God. They love, tend, and make certain of the calling and choosing of each disciple they nurture in their mission of restoration of hearts and lives.

It is by faith that this couple will follow Him no matter where He leads while learning, growing and experiencing changes all along the way in their own hearts and minds. This book is an example of the many hours of teachings that were meant to shake loose and make 'a people' ready for the Lord. The call of restoration is to uproot, tear down, and ruin the works of the enemy by repairing, rebuilding, and restoring hearts and minds through careful tending so as to reveal the heart of the Father to the children. God showed out His intent for fatherhood in the faith through Abraham and even Paul in the New Testament wished many would be fathers in the faith. The faithfulness of God continues to be demonstrated as He raises up Calvin Collins to be not only a pastor, teacher, apostle and any other placement of his calling and giftedness but today, more than ever, a father. This book is a token of love and care for the children of faith.

Carol Ellis
House of Joy

Foreword by Pastor Tony Outlaw

And they that be wise shall shine as the brightness of the firmament; and they that turn many to righteousness as the stars for ever and ever.
Daniel 12:3 (KJV)

We are in a time where the last days are upon us, the earth is being consumed with sin, and the church-in many cases-has shifted from teaching relationship with God, to teaching religion and church philosophy, in order to look the part and mimic the character of Christianity.

Understanding the signs of the times, I am thankful to God for the emergence of the Apostolic/Prophetic gift that Pastor Collins is to the body of the Christ.

With all of the false doctrine and teachings that are ever present within the body, Pastor Collins, has remained a shining example of both the biblical truth and principles, necessary to lead the people of God into God's righteousness and relationship, that make us all effective in witnessing, ministering, and soul winning, as it relates to our kingdom assignments.

Allow this book, "Becoming Spiritual", to minister to your soul, and in doing so, not only will you gain spiritual insight and confirmation of who you are in Christ and the kingdom, but you will assuredly go from religion to relationship, with a clear understanding of biblical truth and Apostolic/Prophetic operation and application.

To God be the glory, for **this** wonderful thing that He has done.

Pastor Tony Outlaw
Bread of Life Worship Church

Preface

When I was twelve years old, and having grown up in poverty and a hustler since the age of seven, I started becoming concerned about the living conditions in my home. My mother raised four boys on her own, with no father in the house, which is the reason I believe times were hard on us towards the end of every month. By the time I was around thirteen years old, I began looking for a way out. I became curious about God and decided to join a Baptist church in Memphis, Tennessee. I quickly began noticing that most of the kids who attended the church flocked together each Sunday, each trying to gain attention from one another. I then started wondering if this was what church was all about for young people. At that point, I started paying attention to what the pastor was teaching. I understood that he was the keynote speaker and the adults who came wanted to hear what he had to say. So I listened to him preaching one Sunday morning. I don't recall exactly what was said, but I knew it wasn't enough to convince me that going to church was the right thing to do.

At the age of 19, I remember visiting my brother who was living and working in Raleigh, North Carolina, and he began sharing the love of Jesus Christ with me. The words that came from his mouth about Jesus brought a sense of relief to me, which is something I did not receive when I joined the first church back in Memphis. It was interesting to know that all of my wrongful ways of living were forgiven and that I could actually start over. As I departed back to my hometown, I could not forget about the things that were on my mind about Jesus Christ. A few more years went by and I found myself up and down at times trying to live a better life. When I would do wrong, I turned to gospel music. When things went well, I enjoyed life, at least for what I thought it was worth, and went back to listening to non positive music again. To make a long story short, I was a very unhappy boy who lacked understanding of how life really worked. Within a one year time span, I returned to Raleigh again to visit my brother for a one week vacation that turned into a twenty-two year stay. I ended up joining a Pentecostal church and this is when my spiritual journey began.

Every Sunday at this church was very exciting to me. No matter how I felt before I got to church, when the service was over, I knew I would feel much better for the rest of that day. The feeling that everything was going to be just fine only lasted a day or so afterwards. I eventually started noticing that I was not the only person feeling this way. My brother, his friends, and the people that I started hanging with were all dealing with some of the same effects. We all would praise God on Sunday, but most often struggled during the week, all the while not understanding and learning from mistakes that we had made just trying to survive. Yet we sang gospel songs with meanings that said things would be better, only to find out later on that we really didn't believe what we were singing about, nor were we experiencing it. Here I was, after four years of living in Raleigh, now ready to pack my bags and move back to Memphis. My mind was made up until a young lady named Kimberly who I had befriended convinced me to stay. We became very close friends and talked about the Lord for hours and hours at a time.

She began pouring into me great things about the Lord which caused my desire to really know the Lord to grow even stronger. Another year or so went by and as I was now growing to trust in the Lord more, my eyes came open and I begin to see the woman of my dreams. It was the same lady that I befriended earlier, my friend Kimberly, who is now my lovely wife for twenty years now. A few years after we were married, **our** lives in terms of what we knew, sang about and live for in the Lord was still not adding up. I ended up resigning from all of my positions in the church and my wife ended up resigning as well. We both came to the agreement that something is missing and we were determined to find out what this something was.

Introduction

After spending seventeen years in only one church, studying the lives of people, and learning from my own mistakes as well as others, the Lord began to deal with me about listening to the Spirit of God on a much different level. For the first time I dared to be and think different than the average Christian. I decided to make the Word more applicable to my life in a more unified way, and oh boy did my relationship with the Lord and among other people improve dramatically.

What inspired me to write this book was God giving me twenty-seven messages under one topic, which was *Becoming Spiritual*. The words shared in this book are key factors in building and laying the foundation for our apostolic-prophetic team that began with myself, wife and kids. God later added a great team of people, most of which God filtered through, to help form a well educated prophetic team. God transitioned us from having years of religion with God to having years of relationship with God. My goal for writing this book is to assist you in leading God's people out of religion of just knowing God exists into having real relationship with God.

This book is dedicated to the Christian, who one day made the same statement I did after discovering something else was missing in my life. Having faithfully been a member of only one Pentecostal church and no other churches over a period of seventeen years, I had come to the conclusion there had to be more in life than this!

This book is purposed to the Christian who wants answers as to why personal issues and problems didn't seem to go away after receiving salvation. This book is for that Christian who never had a true personal experience with God, who has never had a personal relationship with God, who thought that it was not possible to really know God for themselves, who is tired of emoting things inside of their hearts, and don't understand why people continue to say and do bad things. It is for those who have mastered going through repeat patterns of life filled with issues, filled with finger pointing, filled with unhappiness inside, and who are great at suppressing their feelings and hurts that generates negative bodily conditions. They are accustomed to planning for weekly worship, wearing that happy face, shouting, dancing, hearing a Word from the Lord and ending it all by saying "I've had a good time" only to repeat this chain of events week after week and never really growing in the knowledge of Jesus Christ. This book is written to those persons who are ready to rest their minds; who want to know what it is like to live in this world in the manner which God expects them to live, and not necessarily how this world has taught people to hear, see, understand and handle life's challenges. The content of this book has changed my life, my family's life, as well as the saints at Healing and Restoration Discipleship Center (HRDC) who have faithfully trusted and worked with us in building.

God wants to change your life and elevate the average mindset of the Christian who really wants it. This book is your foundation for becoming spiritual in God. This book will direct you in helping you to fulfill your responsibilities as a Christian in this world. It begins with providing details about the purpose of the Holy Spirit, which every Christian should know about and have living inside of them. The Holy Spirit reveals the truth of who God is to people. The Holy Spirit wants to arrest your natural tongue so He can teach you what to say at times, especially difficult times.

This book will teach you about the dangers of trusting in yourself, the importance of letting the Holy Spirit lead you and things you must do to develop your mind into having a real relationship with God. It will also educate you about identifying vital signs in terms of spiritual growth, understanding burdens, defeating the spirits of denial and fear which tend to cripple the spiritual growth of Christians. It will enlighten you about the times that Christians live in today. The principles in *Becoming Spiritual* are just the beginning of something wonderful for you to learn and to know. In Exodus 35:1-3, God told Moses He was going to send to him Bezaleel, a man who God had given special skills to help Moses with building the tabernacle of God. Why because Moses lacked the designing skills that Bezaleel had. God told Moses that I have filled Bezaleel with the Spirit of God, in wisdom, in understanding, in knowledge and in all manner of workmanship to complete the final work building the tabernacle of God. As you are reading this book, I ask that God will fill you with the Spirit of God in wisdom, understanding, knowledge and all manner of workmanship as you begin to build your personal tabernacle of God. I pray that God will send Bezaleel's your way, to help you while in this process of becoming spiritually minded, in the name and by the precious blood of Jesus Christ, Yes and Amen.

Chapter 1-The Purpose of the Holy Spirit

But the Comforter, which is the Holy Ghost, whom the Father will send in my name, he shall teach you all things, and bring all things to your remembrance, whatsoever I have said unto you. - John 14:26

Becoming spiritual is a requirement for every person who claims Jesus Christ as their Lord and Savior. All Christians should know about and have the Holy Spirit living inside of them.

Becoming spiritually minded and having the Holy Spirit goes hand in hand. God expects every Christian to know about and to fully understand the purpose of the Holy Spirit being a part of their lives. The Holy Spirit's presence is a supernatural intervention. It takes faith in God to see and to activate this supernatural intervention in the lives of people. The word intervention means to interfere with the affairs of others so as to modify a process or situation. The word interfere means to come into opposition, to take part in, to strike against or to interpose.

The Holy Spirit was sent into the world by God to bring various types of corrections to all mankind, by daily interfering with the current affairs of men and women, even their actions, in order to modify us into becoming what God has made us to be.

Quench not the Spirit. - 1 Thessalonians 5:19

The Holy Spirit is an active spirit. The word quench means to extinguish or to put out. It means to allow to go out or to suppress. Unlearned Christians time after time continue to extinguish, put out and suppress the working of the Holy Spirit inside of them. Understand it is not wise to quench the instructions and guidance of the Holy Spirit. The Holy Spirit will oppose things that are not of God. This is one of the primary purpose's of the Holy Spirit. The Holy Spirit will inform you of the wrong that you do. The Holy Spirit does not agree with all of what people do, hence the reason why correction is so important to the Christians life. The Holy Spirit will speak against all bad actions. When becoming spiritual in God, you are required to adhere to the changes that the Holy Spirit brings.

Lesson one is that you first believe, accept and learn the ways, leading, and teachings of the Holy Spirit. For beginners, becoming spiritual requires one having the Holy Spirit residing in them and the individual also having a very good understanding of its presence and purpose. No one becomes spiritual without any type of supernatural intervention from God the Father. The Comforter is the Holy Spirit.

What does the word Comforter mean? The Greek meaning for the word Comforter is a calling near or a summons for help. The Holy Spirit is summoned to help us by God the Father. Other attributes of the Comforter are exhortation, admonition, encouragement, consolation, comfort and solace. Comforter is also that which affords comfort or refreshment.

The Holy Spirit was sent to the world from God to bring comfort and refreshment. God's name is in the Holy Spirit. The Holy Spirit will teach people all things that pertain to living life. The Holy Spirit was sent by God to be a part of mankind's daily living. The Holy Spirit will bring exhortation to all who accept Him. Exhortation is to bring comfort, advice, recommendations and warnings.

The purpose of the Holy Spirit is to bring comfort to the Christian believer, to lead them, to assist in building them, to give them advice, to grow them, to give recommendations and bring warnings to them concerning the course of this world.

> *And Jesus being full of the Holy Ghost returned from Jordan, and was led by the Spirit into the wilderness. - Luke 4:1*

When you decide to become spiritual, the Holy Spirit will take you into places for periods of time with a mission of forming and shaping you into who He wants you to become. Jesus was led into the wilderness by the Spirit to be tempted by the devil for a specific period of time.

The first step in becoming spiritual is to learn how to overcome temptation. In the above Scripture, the devil was not tempting Jesus to do anything evil, but tempting Him to come against things that His Father had spoken into His life. The devil was looking for a potential flaw in our Lord to see if he could get Jesus to obey the devil's commandments. To God be the glory this never happened.

When you receive the Holy Spirit, you are getting the fullness of who God is inside of you. There are no flaws in the Holy Spirit.

Let no man say when he is tempted, I am tempted of God: for God cannot be tempted with evil, neither tempted he any man: - James 1:13

God will not tempt you to do something wrong. God will simply allow the temptation to come and let you decide whether or not you will give in to it.

During our Lord's wilderness experience, Jesus was tempted in all points of temptations a person may have. He overcame them all because He was in perfect obedience to his Father. He understood His purpose for being in the world.

In many cases, temptations from the devil can become the average Christians downfall if they don't understand their purpose for being in the world. What would get you to the place of overcoming the enemy's temptations is having perfect obedience to the word of God. Things will begin to change in your mind when you start to work your mind.

The wilderness is a type of human mind. The devil implants various thoughts and ideas into the minds of people. The devil understands the consequences of our choices and knows that most Christians do not. The power Jesus had to overcome temptations and trials resides in those who are filled with the Holy Spirit. The purpose of the Holy Spirit is to teach us how to make the right choices and to overcome the devil's plan for all mankind.

The Holy Spirit provides counsel and advice. Without proper counsel and advice, life can and will be miserable. Miserable lives trigger a certain type of curiosity within the minds of people about various things. If they are truthful with themselves, they are tired and life has beaten them down because they are unable to handle what I call the three big ones of life - fear, anxiety, and stress. Without proper spiritual education, counsel and advice, these three spirits working together in many cases, are designed to deteriorate the lifespan of all human kind which will hinder them in many ways, mostly mentally. It will keep people from fulfilling their God given assignments on Earth.

Before understanding the purpose of the Holy Spirit, one must first accept the fact that God has given them an assignment to complete within the Body of Christ. Once that person has accepted this fact, next they have to be willing to lay down his or her lifestyle of wrongful ways of living that comes as a result of them seeing, hearing and understanding things improperly. A transformation has to take place first in their minds.

There are two main blockages that can hinder this transformation of the mind - tradition and religion. When one is born into the kingdom of God, their journey to becoming spiritual does not begin until the proper training, skills, and understanding are in place. Otherwise, as a Christian, they will continue to find themselves seeing, hearing, and understanding things the same way they did prior to becoming a Christian.

This typical pattern will seduce them into many years of just enjoying church services and having a good time. To become a true Christian, many processes or various deliverances are involved. I know that is shocking to many, but it is absolutely true. Becoming spiritual does not happen automatically. Processes are involved in order for Christians to become spiritual.

To become spiritual, you must put forth some actions. There is an emptying out and a pouring in of things that are mandatory for every Christian to live by.

So what does it mean to become spiritual? To start, the word spiritual itself originated from the Greek word *pneuma*, which simply means a flow of air. An example of *pneuma* is for someone to suddenly receive a breath, a blast, a breeze or a whisk of air. A whisk is something that moves rapidly. So *pneuma* is essentially a "flow of air" that is brought upon something or someone causing it or them to become something or someone else. This *pneuma*, this flow, or this breath of air is also called the Spirit, commonly known as the Holy Spirit. John's Gospel lets us know clearly that God is a Spirit.

> *God is a Spirit: and they that worship him must worship him in spirit and in truth. - John 4:24*

Worshiping God in spirit and in truth is speaking of our human spirit, having been born of and connected to the Holy Spirit with real meaning behind our actions. When we look at the phrase Holy Spirit, the word Holy has to do with having special recognition which means to be sacred.

Anything that is deemed sacred is respected and treated differently from everything else. For God Himself is Holy and sacred. The Holy Spirit is God's breathing Spirit; it is the Holy breath of God. The Holy Spirit is very unique in His operations, unlike any human medical specialists.

The Holy Spirit does His unique operations or transformations in people by reviving the spirit of the humble and the heart of the contrite ones. The Spirit of the living God cannot fully operate with those who suppress Him at times when we need Him the most.

For thus saith the high and lofty One that inhabiteth eternity, whose name is Holy; I dwell in the high and holy place, with him also that is of a contrite and humble spirit, to revive the spirit of the humble, and to revive the heart of the contrite ones. - Isaiah 57:15

The word revive in this Scripture means to make and remain alive; to live again; to have life; to sustain life; to live prosperously and to be restored back to life. The purpose of the Holy Spirit is to revive or to bring back to life the spiritual mindset that men and women once possessed prior to the fall of man.

The mindset prior to the fall of man contained pure and righteous thinking. Without this mindset, the thoughts of men contained iniquitous, unholy, and unrighteous thinking. Not only was their thinking corrupted, their ability to see things from a spiritual perspective became twisted, they began to have a misunderstanding of things due to dull hearing, and their understanding took on a form of worldly confusion. Christians who have not been taught the dependency of the Holy Spirit can still have iniquitous thoughts and a corrupt mindset.

The purpose of the Holy Spirit abiding in Christians is to bring God's spiritual life back into all mankind upon acceptance and proper guidance from Godly spiritual leaders. The Holy Spirit speaks to people in the same manner as you are reading this book in words that you can understand. Once the Holy Spirit is present, the Christian mind is ready for redevelopment and supernatural strength, authority, power, awareness and spiritual insight. Because the Holy Spirit operates in a dimension that He cannot be seen by the visible human eye, it wasn't until we began to read the New Testament writings that the Holy Spirit was called a Ghost.

A ghost is another name for a spirit having the same meaning as *pneuma*, breath, and life. The term Holy Ghost is mostly used in Pentecostal circles. When a person determines they want to become a Christian, they believe this is done by having faith in their mind and believing in their hearts to confess Him as Savior.

The same rule applies to a person who desires to become spiritual. By faith, they receive the Holy breath of God into their natural bodies. It is at this time that they begin their spiritual walk with God. Confessing salvation does not teach you how to be a Christian. Confessing salvation just says that you are a Christian. Learning how to be a spiritual Christian requires assistance from the Holy Spirit or Holy Ghost, in addition to guidance from spiritual servants of God who are apart of Five Fold ministries.

> *And I will give you pastors according to mine heart, which shall feed you with knowledge and understanding. - Jeremiah 3:15*

One of the biggest misconceptions today is the belief that people can know all about God all by themselves. I have been told many times by people that they do not need a pastor, nor a church to attend, and they can just read their Bible themselves and that is all they need. This statement is famous because of a lack of proper Christian teachings in various denominations, which is a lack of knowledge due to a worldly perspective. Sadly they all use the same Bible and all believe in the same God. Ironic isn't it!

The Holy Spirit's purpose is to lead us in the right directions, both spiritually and naturally. The person's mind must be prepared for this type of guidance.

Ever wonder why some Christians who have been saved for a long time still struggle trying to get free from yokes, bondages, habits and burdens? They are burning themselves out doing things they believe are the right thing to do, such as faithfully attending church with hopes of someday seeing a real breakthrough.

Trying to stop doing wrong in your own strength can be a hard thing to do. With the Holy Spirit or Holy Ghost operating freely in you and upon receiving proper biblical education, whatever your hang ups are, overtime, they can be stopped, controlled, and subsequently delivered from your mind or soul. Depending upon the condition of your mind, it may happen instantly.

The Holy Spirit or Holy Ghost, God the Father, and His Son Jesus Christ who is the Word of God, together are one. The Word or Holy Spirit searches the mind and hearts of people once invited to live inside of them. He investigates the damage done to the person's intellect and body as a result of being born into a world filled with choices. The human mind is already conformed to the world's standard of seeing, hearing, and understanding things with and without the presence of God. The Holy Spirit knows where you are hurting the most, where you are dying spiritually, what type of thoughts you have, and what is going on in your mind that funnels the seat of your emotions coming from the heart.

> *For the word of God is quick, and powerful, and sharper than any two-edged sword, piercing even to the dividing asunder of soul and spirit, and of the joints and marrow, and is a discerner of the thoughts and intents of the heart. - Hebrews 4:12*

Many people receive the Holy Ghost in them, but the moment the Holy Ghost tries to get them to do right, their old nature takes control and mentally convinces the Christian to do wrong. The apostle Paul calls this the law of sin. This is another member in our body that wants authority over our mind.

When this law has perfected its work in the mind of people, typically condemnation, guilt, and shame will come forth from the individual. When the Christian learns to respond to the Holy Spirit first, the outcome of every matter will yield positive and promising results.

When you become spiritual, everything you see is no longer seen with your natural eyes. You learn to see things with spiritual eyes. Because of spiritual eyes, your thinking becomes spiritual, meaning God will give you spiritual understanding of things before the natural understanding attempts to come. Most Christians have been taught by the course of this world to accept the natural understanding of things first. This is driven by what I call demonic air assaults.

Wherein in time past ye walked according to the course of this world, according to the prince of the power of the air, the spirit that now works in the children of disobedience: - Ephesians 2:2

The phrase air assault comes from military operation used when flying stealth's. The most common stealth flown is the F-117 Nighthawk. Demonic spirits are likened to F-117 Nighthawk stealth operators.

They are difficult to detect by sight, sound, radar and infrared energies. Demonic stealth operators work the same way. They are secretive and they attack the emotions of people. You will not know what caused you to do or say a thing until it is too late.

Being spiritual will require you to be on high alert to resist demonic air assaults being released into the atmosphere of your current environments. Air assaults are simply reasons, thoughts, ideas and suggestions that come directly from the devil. They come out of nowhere dropping into our mind where we mull over coming to conclusions that lead us to wrong decisions. From my experience, the thoughts may not sound, feel or appear to be demonic, but are designed to pull you away from your purpose in protecting and building yourself up in the things of God.

When you learn to be spiritual, you must learn to recognize demonic air assaults. They come in all forms. Catch them as they come and ensure that the Holy Spirit weighs in on what was released in your mind before you react. The Holy Spirit will inform you right away if it is of God or not.

Timing is another key aspect of being spiritual. Agendas are a huge aspect of God. The Holy Spirit gives His people agendas to follow. Joshua gives us a great example of this.

And they answered Joshua, saying, All that thou commandest us we will do, and whithersoever thou sendest us, we will go. - Joshua 1:16

God had given Joshua a task of leading His people into the Promised Land. Joshua hears the task from God and gives the officers of the people instructions to follow. The officers response to Joshua was all that you command us, we will do and where ever you send us, we will go. As you learn to hear the voice of the Holy Spirit, you are expected to respond the same way by saying: "whatever you command me to do, I will do it and wherever you send me, I will go".

In the Hebrew, Joshua is defined as Jehovah is salvation or the existing One and Yasha which means to save, be saved and be delivered. The name Joshua and Jesus are both common. For each had a goal of bringing prosperity, victory, welfare and deliverance to God's people.

According to Joshua chapters 1-4, we find Joshua guiding and speaking instructions from God to bring His people into the possession of the Promised Land, just as Jesus brings His people to the spiritual or heavenly Canaan or Promised Land through the leading of the Holy Spirit.

> *But when He, the Spirit of Truth (the Truth-giving Spirit) comes, He will guide you into all the Truth (the whole, full Truth). For He will not speak His own message [on His own authority]; but He will tell whatever He hears [from the Father; He will give the message that has been given to Him], and He will announce and declare to you the things that are to come [that will happen in the future]. - John 16:13 (Amplified Version)*
>
> *For if Jesus had given them rest, then would he not afterward have spoken of another day. – Hebrews 4:8*

For this reason, Joshua has been regarded as a type of Christ and Holy Spirit because he essentially did what Jesus did to bring people to a place of rest.

I recall something that happened to me recently where the Holy Spirit reminded me of an agenda that I was given by God. I had a synopsis to write concerning Healing and Restoration Discipleship

Center (HRDC) and found myself putting it off for several days. When I purposed in my heart to begin to complete the synopsis, an air assault came to my mind to listen to a very good pastor's sermon on compact disk (CD) that was good in building my spirit up as well. This thought came to my mind as I was driving home from work. So when I got home, I began listening to the CD. Shortly thereafter, the Holy Spirit said "Calvin, the synopsis!" I immediately stopped what I was doing and began to finish my synopsis. The Holy Spirit at that time gave me powerful, prophetic words and revelations to write in the synopsis that did not come in times past.

It was then that I realized that demonic air assaults can cause you to do other things "that are designed to build you up in God" and potentially cause you to miss receiving fresh revelation needed to complete an agenda in your life. The air assault did not sound demonic, but it was designed to block the fresh words of prophesy coming from God at that time. When you learn to be spiritually minded, the Holy Spirit will teach you how to overcome, win and to cast down these types of air assaults. Demonic air assaults can also program people to think they know and understand more than God Himself.

The Holy Spirit, when allowed to operate in people, will help them see things from a different yet spiritual perspective. This is what gives the Christian an edge on everyday living, which the non-Christian or Christian who is not spirit-filled cannot understand.

> *For what man knoweth the things of a man, save (except) the spirit of man which is in him? Even so the things of God knoweth no man, but the Spirit of God. Now we have received, not the spirit of the world, but the spirit which is of God; that we might*

know the things that are freely given to us of God. - 1 Corinthians 2:11-12

The Holy Spirit gives the believer wisdom to do things and the understanding of all things. A Christian who has been taught to understand the Holy Spirit from a religious aspect will struggle to get this. When I speak of a religious aspect, I am making reference to an individual who has been programmed to only see and view God in mostly non-personal ways. They only see and view God from their pastor's or denominational perspective in terms of how he or she thinks of God. They rarely think of knowing God in a more intimate way themselves. A spirit of fear blocks them from going down this path.

A Christian who has been taught to understand the Holy Spirit from a relationship aspect will excel in Godly wisdom and understanding. A person whose mind is relationship driven is open for prophetic insight and instructions. When a person has a strong daily relationship with God in their lives with the guidance of the Holy Spirit or Holy Ghost, they will have no problem becoming spiritual. They automatically begin to yield themselves over to spirit filled believers who can pour into them kingdom knowledge. They are ready to accept God's order, judgment, administration and establishment through the pastor who has an apostolic anointing.

Apostolic is a word used to describe the teachings and workings of an apostle. The attributes of an apostle is to pioneer, govern, establish, administer, set boundaries, take territories, bring order, bring deliverance, bring clear vision, preach and teach with unique styles.

Apostles are anointed by God to do this work. Apostolic anointing brings relief, justice, freedom and comfort to God's people.

Apostles rely heavily on the Holy Spirit to do this work because the Holy Spirit is an apostolic spirit. The Holy Spirit is apostolic because He is sent by God.

> *But the Comforter, which is the Holy Ghost, whom the Father will send in my name, he shall teach you all things, and bring all things to your remembrance, whatsoever I have said unto you. - John 14:26*

When you begin to study the Word of God for yourself through relationship aspects and not religious, when you begin to listen often to apostolic teachings, when you begin to experience prophetic worship, you are well on your way to a more driven purpose of understanding the importance of having the Holy Spirit living inside of you.

Apostolic teachings consist of the teachings and working of the first apostles.

> *And they continued stedfastly in the apostles' doctrine and fellowship, and in breaking of bread, and in prayers. - Acts 2:42*

The word prophetic means to hear the voice of God clearly and to respond to that voice in a truthful way. Prophetic worship allows you to seriously take to heart what God is speaking and respond accordingly. Apostolic teachings and prophetic worship are key principles in becoming spiritual in God.

I pray for those Christians who have not received the gift of the Holy Ghost. I issue a decree that they will be directed to prophetic people who are connected to deliverance ministries where they can receive the Holy Spirit and be taught properly how to grow in the knowledge and grace of God. The Holy Ghost will develop your new life in the Lord. The Holy Ghost will protect you from hurt, harm, and danger. The Holy Spirit will benefit those who are willing and ready to lay down their old ways of seeing, hearing, understanding, thinking and living so they may truly become spiritual.

Chapter 2-The Spirit Reveals Things to Us

But God hath revealed them unto us by his Spirit: for the Spirit searches all things, yes, the deep things of God. - 1 Corinthians 2:10

God wants to reveal deep things about Himself to you through the Holy Spirit. The Holy Spirit searches all things about you, including both the good and the bad, and reveals these things to your human spirit. As you are becoming spiritual, the Holy Spirit will reveal the wrong that you do. This is not the time to reject these things. The Holy Spirit will reveal them to you in visions, dreams, the word and gifts of the Spirit.

Have you ever wondered why in the world you keep doing certain things repeatedly? Have you ever asked yourself how did this begin? The Holy Spirit can reveal to you the root cause of these matters including things that were even a part of your ancestors in past generations. The Holy Spirit reveals answers to everything. To really know the Holy Spirit, you must be filled with the Holy Spirit.

And the LORD spake unto Moses, saying, see, I have called by name Bezaleel the son of Uri, the son of Hur, of the tribe of Judah. And I have filled him with the spirit of God, in wisdom, and in understanding, and in knowledge, and in all manner of workmanship. - Exodus 31:1-3

The wisdom, understanding, knowledge and all manner of workmanship skills that were given to Bezaleel are attributes of the Holy Spirit. Bezaleel was picked by God to assist Moses in putting the finishing touches on the building of God's tabernacle. Bezaleel was prepared by God to do this work.

There is a finished work that we must do to become the person God made us to be. The Holy Spirit enables us to become that finished work by giving us wisdom, understanding, knowledge and special skills. Bezaleel's experience in workmanship came as a result of him being filled with the Spirit of God.

Christian skills are built as a result of being filled with the Spirit of God. When you are not filled with the Spirit of God, you learn no new skills and fighting techniques. The Holy Spirit cannot reveal new skills and fighting techniques into your mind. Because Bezaleel was filled with the Spirit of God, he acquired skills to work with wood, stones, and clay.

Bezaleel is a type of the Holy Spirit. In Exodus 35:1-3, God told Moses he was going to send to him Bezaleel, a man who God had given special skills to help Moses with building the tabernacle of God. Why, because Moses lacked the designing skills that Bezaleel had.

As a Christian without the Holy Spirit, you lack designing skills in building your spiritual house, hence the importance of having the Holy Spirit. Jesus told His disciples in **Luke 24:49 (New Living Translation) - And now I will send the Holy Spirit, just as my Father promised. But stay here in the city until the Holy Spirit comes and fills you with power from heaven.**

God told Moses that I have filled Bezaleel with the Spirit of God, in wisdom, in understanding, in knowledge and in all manner of workmanship to complete the final work building the tabernacle of God. Your human body is a temple that the Holy Spirit wishes to abide in so He can fill you with the designing skills which was given to Bezaleel.

> *Do you not know that your body is the temple (the very sanctuary) of the Holy Spirit Who lives within you, Whom you have received [as a Gift] from God? You are not your own. - 1 Corinthians 6:19 (Amplified Version)*

What was placed inside of Bezaleel is also found in the Holy Spirit. Having the Holy Spirit actively working in you will give you the anointing to change your life and provide a clean place for the Holy Spirit to dwell in. God wants to make you a completed work with the best of what He has to offer. God does not want you to remain an uncompleted work, which is a Christian who has not accepted their full birthright or what you are entitled to.

You must desire to have a real relationship with the Lord and be willing to become sensitive to the heart and mind of God in order to take full advantage of what the Holy Spirit has to offer. If you are in search for peace in life, be mindful that the course of this world has taught people to look for peace in all the wrong places.

The Holy Spirit can reveal the signs of this wicked behavior that is present in their lives. People who are not filled with the Holy Spirit tend to not notice these signs which is the reason why God knew most people would not turn from their wicked ways easily on their own.

This is why He sent into the world the Holy Spirit, to assist people in turning from their wicked ways. What made your ways wicked consisted of how you saw, heard, and understood things with your natural eyes, ears and mind. The purpose for the Holy Spirit being in your life is to challenge, to come against or to oppose this in you. The Holy Spirit is not optional, but a necessity for your life as a Christian. The Holy Spirit is a major part of the foundation of being a Christian.

And they were all filled with the Holy Ghost, and began to speak with other tongues, as the Spirit gave them utterance. - Acts 2:4

Notice in the above Scripture that after people are filled with the Holy Ghost or Spirit, the next thing the Christian does is to begin speaking with other tongues as the Spirit gives them utterance. Utterance is to have the ability to speak out or to speak forth things from your mouth. The other tongues are new words that your spirit is speaking directly from the Holy Spirit to God.

For one who speaks in an [unknown] tongue speaks not to men but to God, for no one understands or catches his meaning, because in the [Holy] Spirit he utters secret truths and hidden things [not obvious to the understanding].
1 Corinthians 14:2 (Amplified Version)

These new tongues are to be released out of your mouth frequently as you are growing spiritually, especially in your personal development, prayer and devotional time with God. The Holy Spirit will reveal mysteries to your spirit man when you are speaking unknown tongues. The mysteries would consist of all truths, things present and future things pertaining to your life and others that are given to the Holy Spirit by God.

> *He who speaks in a [strange] tongue edifies and improves himself, but he who prophesies [interpreting the divine will and purpose and teaching with inspiration] edifies and improves the church and promotes growth [in Christian wisdom, piety, holiness, and happiness].*
> *1 Corinthians 14:4 (Amplified Version)*

The unknown or strange tongue when spoken frequently edifies or charges the believer up such as how a battery charges. The more tongues you speak, the longer you stay charged up. This standard practice will increase your faith to continually believe God.

You're always charged up on God's power source daily when speaking unknown tongues. This will enable you to have supernatural strength, spiritual maturation and promote growth in your personal relationship with God.

Speaking unknown tongues is the initial evidence or sign of the Baptism of the Holy Spirit and is the beginning of the spirit life training. Speaking in unknown tongues as often as possible should be the basic foundational principal for believers. For this is the supernatural source of power for our everyday life.

The Holy Spirit and new tongues are signs that God is with you. They depict who Jesus Christ is to the world. The world in many cases despises Christians whose lifestyle does not depict Jesus Christ. This is because they have not been filled with the Holy Spirit. Their Christian lifestyles without the Holy Spirit have caused the hearts of men and women to consider other alternatives to God. This came as a result of the ignorance and ideology of men and lack of proper biblical teaching.

Receiving the Holy Spirit is a mandate straight from God. All Christians MUST receive the Holy Spirit. Christians will find it difficult to reach their full potential in God without the Holy Spirit properly abiding and working in them daily. If you do not have the Holy Spirit, my prayer is that you receive Him now. Living is hard without Him.

> *And it came to pass, that, while Apollos was at Corinth, Paul having passed through the upper coasts came to Ephesus: and finding certain disciples, he said unto them, Have ye received the Holy Ghost since ye believed? And they said unto him, We have not so much as heard whether there be any Holy Ghost. - Acts 19:1-2*

When I first received the Holy Spirit, I have to be honest, not much changed in my life in terms of making better decisions. I stopped living life as a sinner and began thinking about God more, but as far as personal traits, understandings, guidance, direction, decision making, these things DID NOT improve. They remained the same as a Christian. Wow. This was all because I lacked understanding of where God had taken me. I was told to simply get saved, and as a result, all of my problems would go away and I would have a one way ticket to heaven. Due to this lack of understanding, my problems increased and I was ready to head back to my home Memphis. All I knew was to suppress my issues, go to church and have a good time, only to repeat the cycle for months and months, which turned into years.

I did not know nor understood the power of the Holy Spirit in me. The course of this world kept me from trying to understand why. Air assaults would block my mind from ever wondering what it would be like. My salvation was dependent solely on the pastor. I eventually realized I needed to be cultivated in order for change to begin. Some critical thinking had to take place. There were things I needed to do in order for change to happen.

Becoming a new person in Christ is not an automatic process just by you saying Lord save me and fill me with the Holy Ghost. Absolutely not! There is work that you have to do. There is a process you must go through. If you grew up with a lazy mentality, the basics of salvation are all you will ever know until you break free from this lazy mentality.

You need to be a part of a deliverance ministry to understand clearly the basics of salvation and next steps in gaining control over your life. If you want to thrive in the wisdom and understanding of God, break out the midnight oil because there is much work to do. The Holy Spirit cannot reveal Himself fully to people who are lazy in terms of not wanting to read, not just the Bible, but even spiritual books to gain insight about God.

In the sweat of thy face shalt thou eat bread, till thou return unto the ground; for out of it wast thou taken: for dust thou art, and unto dust shalt thou return. - Genesis 3:19

The word bread in this text comes from the Hebrew word *lechem*. *Lechem* was originated from the word law-cham, which means to fight, to do battle, to make war.

The English word generated from *lechem* is lectern. Dictionary.com defines lectern as a reading desk in a church on which the Bible rests and is used for study purposes.

> *I am that bread of life. Your fathers did eat manna in the wilderness, and are dead. This is the bread which cometh down from heaven, that a man may eat thereof, and not die. - John 6:48-50*

Jesus makes reference to the Word of God as the bread of life. Jesus is that bread. The Word of God is the bread. The Word became flesh and dwelt among the people.

> *But he answered and said, It is written, Man shall not live by bread alone, but by every word that proceedeth out of the mouth of God.*
> *- Matthew and Luke 4:4*

Jesus said man shall not live by bread alone, but by every word that proceeded out of the mouth of God, and right here He was again speaking of spiritual bread. So if I were to read Genesis 3:19 in the prophetic, it will say...In the sweat of thy face shall thou be very busy reading.

It is here that God was sending a clear message out to all mankind saying, whoever is looking to truly become spiritual in God and to have the Holy Spirit reveal Himself and things to them on a personal level, they will have to put in long hours and work extremely hard. That person's goal is to regain the spiritual mindset of seeing, hearing, and understanding things properly as it was prior to the fall of man. This task is done through reading books, listening to messages over and over, fasting and praying strategic prayers. This is likened to one being resurrected from the dead, but from the perspective of being only spiritually dead in knowledge.

You will have to fight, do battle, and rage war in your mind against the flesh. And with the assistance of the Holy Spirit, you can win and come against the wrong perception in seeing, hearing, and misunderstanding things. To accomplish this task, you must see this as something mandatory. Initially you may not believe this can be done, but it can.

> *But ye shall receive power, after that the Holy Ghost is come upon you: and ye shall be witnesses unto me both in Jerusalem, and in all Judaea, and in Samaria and unto the uttermost part of the earth.*
> *- Acts 1:8*

The power that the Holy Spirit reveals is the ability to make things happen that might seem impossible to the natural eyes. The people that lived in Jerusalem, Judea, and Samaria were the first to have the Holy Ghost revealed to them in a supernatural way. God knew that as a result of wrong living, sin in the world, and people lacking this power of the Holy Spirit, they were at great risk of their lives being messed up, tied up, and tangled up in all kinds of problems and issues. In order to understand this second chapter, I strongly encourage you to clearly understand the first chapter of this book entitled "The Purpose of the Holy Spirit" so that you can understand clearly what God wants you to hear directly from His heart concerning us being the body of Christ. Amen.

The average Christian who says they are Spirit filled has done a poor job comforting, nurturing, and developing a new believer. This is because they do not understand they are going through a process of transformation as well. Christians assume they are ready right away to bring deliverance to someone else. In reality they are not.

There is much that the average Christian must learn. The Holy Spirit brings comfort and style to those He works with.

> *And I will pray the Father, and he shall give you another Comforter, that he may abide with you forever; - John 14:16*

When Jesus was in the world, He was that comforter, which was a person who was with them every step of the way while transforming their lives. He now speaks in the future that when He leaves, He will send us another Comforter, which is another name for the Holy Spirit.

The word Comforter in the Greek comes from the word *Parakletos* which means to have someone additional on our side as our judge; our pleader; our assistant and our helper. This Comforter we cannot physically see with our own eyes because He is a Spirit that abides in the spirit of man, woman, boy or girl.

Family and friends will wonder what happened to you because you are doing and saying weird things now. Trust me, they will not understand until they are willing to accept Christ and be willing to change themselves. It will be difficult for them to accept this lifestyle as being true, hence why the Holy Spirit is also known as the Spirit of truth.

> *Even the Spirit of truth; whom the world cannot receive, because it sees him not, neither knows him: but ye know him; for he dwells with you, and shall*

> *be in you. I will not leave you comfortless: I will come to you. - John 14:17-18*

Having said this, there should be a difference in the lifestyle of someone who claims to be a Christian in contrast to someone who does not claim to be a Christian. The non-Christian should never see two types of Christians, one who is Spirit filled and does not know what he or she possesses inside of them and the other one not Spirit filled, and say they are both the same. The non-Christian will see no difference in how they are living and simply choose to live life the way they have always known.

The church body should never become known as a body of people who live, see, hear, understand, and think with the same mindset of people who are not saved. In order for the Spirit to reveal Himself in us, as Christians, we must receive this *Parakletos*, which is the Holy Ghost; otherwise we lack the power that we need in order to bring about a change in our lives and others.

> *And it came to pass, that, while Apollos was at Corinth, Paul having passed through the upper coasts came to Ephesus: and finding certain disciples. He said unto them, Have ye received the Holy Ghost since ye believed? And they said unto him, We have not so much as heard whether there be any Holy Ghost. - Acts 19:1-2*

Paul understood these disciples indeed were lacking something very important in their lives that Jesus said they will need in order to survive in this life. As we learned in Chapter 1, a ghost is another name for a spirit having the same meaning of *pneuma*, breath, and life. People receive the gift of the Holy Ghost by faith into their human spirit which resides in the natural body.

> *Jesus saith unto her (being Mary Magdalene), Woman, why weepest thou? whom seekest thou? She, supposing him to be the gardener, saith unto him, Sir, if thou have borne him hence, tell me where thou hast laid him, and I will take him away. Jesus saith unto her, Mary. She turned herself, and saith unto him, Rabboni; which is to say, Master. - John 20:15-16 (emphasis added)*

Not long after our Lord was raised from the dead, He returned again to the same place where they had laid him down in the grave. Mary was having a conversation with two angels clothed in white linen informing them that men had taken the body of Jesus away. As she was speaking, she turned around and looked once and did not recognize Jesus standing behind her. She thought Jesus was a stranger, and called him Sir. Jesus asked her what was wrong. She explained her story again, turned away from Jesus and then back to Jesus again and this time she recognized who the Lord was, and called him Master.

There are millions of Christians who have received the Holy Spirit, but nothing has really changed in their lives. Many never think to question why has not anything changed for the better. If this is you, nothing will change for you until you understand Who you now have living inside of you. You must educate yourself about the Holy Spirit. Mary's eyes were opened the moment she took the time to understand Who was talking to her.

You should ask yourself, "What have I been missing out on?" Mary ran and told the other disciples that she had seen the Lord, but no disciple made any attempts to go see for themselves for fear that the Jews would find them.

Religious people operate like this today. They may appear to be happy for you because of your pursuit of the Holy Spirit, but will not look to investigate for themselves.

People who are relationship driven will desire to know the Holy Spirit personally also. When Jesus came, this was a sign of the Holy Spirit revealing Himself to Mary and others in a spiritual way.

> *Then said Jesus to them again, Peace be unto you: as my Father hath sent me, even so send I you. And when he had said this, he breathed on them, and saith unto them, Receive ye the Holy Ghost: - John 20:21-22*

When the Holy Spirit comes, He brings peace with Him which takes root in the human spirit of the person. Rest is another word for peace. Sabbath is another word for peace. Shalom is another word for peace.

The Holy Spirit will bring rest or Shalom to your mind concerning all matters of life. People will suspect something is wrong with you when you truly make a decision to become spiritual. They may say you are too deep or very religious. You are neither.

Spiritual people enjoy spending quality time with God, regardless if they are in a public facility such as a church or ministry or in the comfort of their own homes. Spiritual people understand they need to be well educated before assisting someone else in getting deliverance. This process can take years of perfecting. The humble in spirit will be rewarded greatly by God. So whether people receive the Holy Ghost by breath or by the laying on of hands, the

Holy "*Pneuma*" Ghost begins the process of old things passing away and all things becoming new.

Becoming spiritual gives the born again believer a new beginning. The Holy Spirit will reveal to you new things, things you may have never ever heard of, but they make a lot of good common sense.

Chapter 3-Knowing What To Say in Hard Times

For the Holy Ghost shall teach you in the same hour what ye ought to say. - Luke 12:12

One of the many assets of being filled with the Holy Ghost or Spirit is that you will not be left speechless at important times in your life. You will always speak the right things when you engage the Holy Spirit for help. When you are living a sanctified, consecrated, set apart and different life from everyone else, the Holy Spirit will release to you from the third heaven the right words to say or pray. Third heaven is symbolic of the place where God resides in the heavenlies.

> *I knew a man in Christ above fourteen years ago, (whether in the body, I cannot tell; or whether out of the body, I cannot tell: God knows;) such an one caught up to the third heaven. - 2 Corinthians 12:2*

Paul makes reference to a man that he knew of about (14) years ago. This man spoke words from the third heaven. His words were very prophetic, meaning as he heard God speaking these words, he responded only to what God said. These words were full of prophecy, meaning they revealed the truth of who God is and His will for all mankind.

Satan can speak words that may appear are coming from the third heaven. His words may not appear to be or sound bad, but in some kind of crafty way, it's designed to stop the flow of prophecy. This is called second heaven revelation. Deliverance ministries can teach you how to detect this kind of word.

When you are not allowing the Holy Spirit to govern your human spirit as it is connected to the Holy Spirit, you can be at risk of speaking things about God from second heaven revelation. When the hard times do arrive, your words may not provide the right kind of impact to invoke change. As you are becoming spiritual in God, the Holy Spirit will teach you what to say at the right times.

One of the most common oversights among Christians is they're not understanding the function of the Holy Spirit. To start, the Holy Spirit's primary role is to lead and to guide us into all truths of life.

The Holy Spirit is the Spirit of truth. Truth is defined as what is true in any matter under consideration. It has to do with reality, fact and certainty. Truth is what is true in things pertaining to God and the duties of man.

The Holy Spirit will bring you into the reality of things. He will bring to your attention all important facts needed in making decisions. The Holy Spirit will give us a certainty of things as they are presented to us. The Holy Spirit will bring supernatural intervention your way whenever you need it most.

God brings correction in order to perfect man. God has always been concerned about the welfare of people in this world. He had a well thought out plan in mind to deliver His people from all kinds of problems. God's plan is to teach people what to say when faced with personal decisions.

> *Howbeit when he, the Spirit of truth, is come, he will guide you into all truth: for he shall not speak of himself; but whatsoever he shall hear, that shall he speak: and he will show you things to come. -*
> *John 16:13*

Before the Spirit of truth came into the world, most men relied on what was programmed into their minds in terms of how they saw, understood, and heard things concerning life. This mindset is as a result of many styles of religion in the world today.

There are people today that say they believe in God and will refute the fact that having the Holy Spirit operating in their lives is a major part of being a Christian. However, there is a dependency and trust factor that plays a major role in the Christian's life concerning the Holy Spirit. There are many religions with various teachings about the Holy Spirit. When understood and taught properly, the Holy Spirit will give you the proper verbiage when answers are needed and in making decisions.

There are times when we are faced with situations that require a proper response. The Spirit of truth, which is the Holy Spirit, will tell the truth about humans. If you have personal issues in your life that affect how you feel about yourself and others, the Spirit of truth will give insight to you. This insight is not designed for you to reject, but to accept, as this is God's way of correcting the wrong that resides in us.

The Holy Spirit's function is to give you what to say during these moments along with directions and guidance on how to resolve these matters.

When the Holy Spirit speaks to you, you will understand what is being spoken to you. The words will come to you just as simple as you are reading this book.

How many times have we heard someone speaking to us and we simply gave the wrong response because we thought we knew the answer already? You must train yourself to not allow your emotions to speak first, but to depend on the Holy Spirit's help to understand what is being spoken to you and then release what the Holy Spirit would have you to say. This method can and will protect you from releasing carnal statements or views.

There are different views from various church denominations that detail the life of a Christian and the Holy Spirit. There are churches that do not believe in the Holy Spirit yet they teach from the Holy Bible, and churches that believe in a Spirit, but dare not call it a Holy Spirit. So where does this place the Christian who discovers the Scriptures which describes the functions of the Holy Spirit?

It will place them in a precarious position when they find themselves struggling with what they can or cannot say, to not be ostracized by people who are against this lifestyle.

You will be in situations where help is needed. You will want an understanding of things. You will seek direction. This book is designed to steer you in that direction.

Being a part of a ministry that does not teach the essence, value, and importance of the Holy Spirit will keep you in the dark about many things. That is why our Lord sent the Holy Spirit into the world. He knew we could not make it on our own without some type of supernatural assistance.

Nevertheless I tell you the truth; It is expedient for you that I go away: for if I go not away, the Comforter will not come unto you; but if I depart, I will send him unto you. - John 16:7

It is a part of God's plan for all human kind to have a divine intervention with them for the rest of their lives. It is the believers' only real chance of completely fulfilling God's plan for their lives.

Without the Holy Spirit abiding in us, we are not able to function spiritually because we lack seeing, hearing and understanding things spiritually. It is important that the believer's spirit remains humble also. Yielding yourself to the guidance of the Holy Spirit is the key to your success.

The Holy Spirit does not see, hear, understand nor think the way a natural person would. His cognition of things surpasses how the human mind thinks and responds because He comes directly from God. God wants to train us to think this way which takes commitment, practice and great understanding. Pastors must teach their members how to do this.

Without the proper teaching, millions of Christians will continue to live life programmed to think and to respond in various ways that are contrary to the teachings of the Holy Spirit. These people will continue to live lives not knowing how to handle things properly.

If we grew up without a real relationship with God in terms of knowing how to depend on Him for guidance, we will automatically rely on what we know based on how we were taught by parents, the culture we live in and by the religious sects we are involved in. Again, if this is all we know, we will continue to respond this way until proper education is given.

For my thoughts are not your thoughts, neither are your ways my ways, saith the LORD. For as the heavens are higher than the earth, so are my ways higher than your ways, and my thoughts than your thoughts. - Isaiah 55:9-10

Every way of a man is right in his own eyes: but the LORD pondereth the hearts - Proverbs 21:2

What continues to be a trend today if proper education is not given on the Holy Spirit is iniquitous thinking. When iniquitous thinking is present, iniquitous responses will follow. People will respond based on how their minds were programmed from birth, on through childhood and well into their adulthood.

If the basic principles of Christianity and the Holy Ghost are not properly taught, people will continue to have a conformed mindset which does not fully understand God. They will continue to see what they do or say as right in their own eyes. With this type of thinking, the odds of them responding properly can be very slim unless they find a deliverance ministry as referred to in chapter one.

People who lack a deliverance ministry will find it hard to submit to apostolic authority. They will have a hard time accepting others who are becoming spiritual as well.

I have been a Christian now for twenty-five years and I have seen many Christians still operating with this same mindset. Their minds are fixed and settled on what "they believe" God wants them to do as a Christian. And when they are challenged to think outside the box to develop "a new understanding" of what God desires them to do, some often refuse to do so.

And all of us, as with unveiled face, [because we] continued to behold [in the Word of God] as in a mirror the glory of the Lord, are constantly being transfigured into His very own image in ever increasing splendor and from one degree of glory to another; [for this comes] from the Lord [Who is] the Spirit. 2 Corinthians 3:18(Amplified Version)

Based on the above Scripture, you are expected to continually grow in grace and in the knowledge of God. God should not be limited in your understanding of Him.

Many pastors avoid scriptural teachings on the Holy Ghost because of controversial issues such as unknown tongues and holy living. They have taught people they can have God and still live life any way they want to. Eventually, these pastors will ban their members from speaking or teaching on the Holy Spirit.

I have met people who were thrown out of ministries because they dared to teach on the Holy Spirit. They were found guilty by men who thought different. Dealing with guilt can be both bad and good at times.

A typical Christian will rely on what comes to mind first because they do not understand fully the purpose of the Holy Spirit. Every Christian who receives the Holy Spirit will have to develop patience in their lives. Patience allows the Holy Spirit to reveal messages to us on time.

But when they deliver you up, take no thought how or what ye shall speak: for it shall be given you in that same hour what ye shall speak.
- Matthew 10:19

If you never learn to depend on the counsel and guidance of the Holy Spirit, you will feel bad about every wrong response. When properly taught and you have a full understanding of the purpose of the Holy Spirit, you will be grateful for every opportunity that comes your way.

Guilt will sometimes bring what's wrong back to our attention and it has to be handled properly. Guilt is designed to steer you in the right direction to learn from your mistakes. If this is misunderstood, guilt can take you down the path of condemning yourself severely for making wrong statements. You must avoid this fatal mistake as it can hinder your growth and walk with the Lord.

Conviction is designed for Christians to learn how to improve their actions and responses, not to dwell on the actions and responses in shame. Conviction comes from God. Condemnation, guilt and shame come from the enemy. When these three are prolonged in a person's life, they can become an issue bringing unhealthy conditions to the body, both naturally and spiritually.

As the Holy Ghost begins to teach us and give us things to do, we will remain on track to becoming better people. The more you depend, hunger and thirst to be filled with the Holy Spirit and the more you desire to become spiritual in God, the Holy Spirit will continue to give you things to say. When you meet a Christian who has little to say about the Holy Spirit, here is a Christian who doesn't understand the purpose of the Holy Spirit.

The Holy Spirit is our reliability agent and is someone you can count on for directions during good and bad times of life. The Holy Spirit is accurate, honest, and dependable.

> *In everything give thanks: for this is the will of God in Christ Jesus concerning you.*
> *- 1 Thessalonians 5:18*

The Holy Spirit will never lead you down the wrong path. If the Holy Spirit gives you a decision to make and it does not turn out the way YOU may think it should, still trust the Holy Spirit's guidance. The Holy Spirit knows the outcome. Do not go back to doing things your way.

Do not allow others to convince you to believe you are better off handling things according to how the course of this world teaches. People who resist change for themselves should not have the last say for your life. They will try to control your future if you let them. Your dependency must be on God.

God is the only One who controls your future. If God tells you to make a change, you're better off obeying God and not being concerned with what people have to say about your direction. His purpose is change your life first and then the lives of others.

> *And when they bring you unto the synagogues, and unto magistrates, and powers, take ye no thought how or what thing ye shall answer, or what ye shall say. For the Holy Ghost shall teach you in the same hour what ye ought to say. - Luke 12:11-12*

As you are becoming spiritual, you must depend on God, the Holy Spirit and your pastor's spiritual guidance and instructions to learn properly. You must remember that becoming spiritual is a process. You must humble yourselves to the authority of those whom God has placed over you to teach you this process.

Always ask questions of those who are skilled with this knowledge. Always honor their spiritual guidance among yourselves and others, so as not to cause a split in the church body that can open the doors for division, murmuring and complaining to upset camp.

You must remember you are the one being taught. You have a life to live with just you and the Holy Spirit. You can choose to accept the Holy Spirit's advice or continue to live a hard life as a Christian.

Chapter 4-The Danger of Trusting In Ourselves

But we had the sentence of death in ourselves, that we should not trust in ourselves, but in God which raise the dead. - 2 Corinthians 1:9

The key phrase in the above Scripture is that we should not trust in ourselves. When people begin to learn and understand what it means to be a Christian and actually start the process of becoming spiritual, just know that all kinds of things may happen preventing them from doing the right thing.

People will trust their first instinct towards things because this is what they are accustomed to doing. When we react on our first instinct, we react out of our emotions before thinking about the subject. There is a danger of responding from our emotions first.

The Holy Spirit will teach you how to acknowledge Him first when you are tasked with giving a response. The right responses are always present with you each time you allow your spirit to respond with the guidance from the Holy Spirit.

Using this method, you will learn to have time to think about certain subjects before releasing words into the atmosphere. Our emotions can cause us to respond inappropriately when they are not managed properly. Unmanaged emotions will program people to depend more on what they can see rather than how the emotions make them feel.

> *What? know ye not that your body is the temple of the Holy Ghost which is in you, which ye have of God, and ye are not your own?- 1 Corinthians 6:19*

Our bodies are the temple of the Holy Spirit. It is the Holy Spirit's job to assist us in redeveloping of ourselves to become that spiritual believer. But as the Holy Spirit is moving, sometimes our emotions get in the way and block His progressive work in us.

You must understand your body does not belong to you anymore once you become a Christian. Therefore you should not trust the bodily wants and desires if they do not line up with the Word of God. The Holy Spirit knows exactly what's needed to build His temple inside of us. The temple represents God's dwelling place. God wants to dwell in you at all times to ensure you are not depending on your natural life to survive in this world. But understand this can be the fight of your life because you are accustomed to doing things your way.

The challenge that a new Christian faces when they make a decision to live for God is building themselves up with the truth of God's Word. They have to hear God's word being taught well and implement immediate action plans that will assist them into becoming spiritual. In addition they have to involve themselves in much personal studying, and be given to much prayer and fasting in order to build themselves up in God.

> *But ye, beloved, building up yourselves on your most holy faith, praying in the Holy Ghost, Keep yourselves in the love of God, looking for the mercy of our Lord Jesus Christ unto eternal life.*
> *– Jude 1:20-21*

Jude was an Apostle who also worked with Paul. He made mention of us as building ourselves up on our most holy faith. The apostolic (apo-stolic) or apostle like teachings and works are what are building the lives of true Christians today. Apostolic teachers teach people how to pray in the Holy Ghost or Spirit.

Prophets provide ongoing encouragement, exhortation and edification to Christians as they learn to do things by the Spirit.

> *What is it then? I will pray with the spirit, and I will pray with the understanding also: I will sing with the spirit, and I will sing with the understanding also. - 1 Corinthians 14:15*

> *Likewise the Spirit also helps our infirmities: for we know not what we should pray for as we ought: but the Spirit itself make intercession for us with groanings which cannot be uttered - Romans 8:26*

Spiritual people pray with words revealed to them by God that are easily understood and they pray in unknown tongues as the Spirit makes intercession on their behalf to God. Spiritual people are determined to stay real for God. They anticipate the arrival of God's mercy resting upon their lives. They know if they rely on their emotions or flesh to lead them, they have exposed themselves allowing the enemy to take possession of their minds.

Bottom line here is that we are not to put any dependence in our flesh, especially when we know one moment when things are going well, we are focused on what God is doing in us and on things that we are to do for Him, and then all of a sudden strange things begin to happen just to take our attention off what God is doing in our lives.

Paul was a traveling man who was busy establishing churches. Paul rarely traveled alone. In one case, Paul and Timothy were scheduled to pass through the city Corinth while on their way back to Macedonia to meet another brother in the Lord by the name of Titus.

Paul had one goal in mind upon arrival to Macedonia, which was to provide words of comfort and advice to the saints there and to also correct some Jewish teachers who had begun to lead the saints into the direction of living life as a Christian, but not according to the New Covenant teachings given by the apostles. These Jewish teachers held strongly to their traditions and religious practices. They were against anyone who was in the business of being cross-trained away from the Old Covenant teachings.

Biblical history informs us that this type of cross-training has been going on for quite some time, even in the times that we are living in now. It is a part of the apostolic movement that you will find this type of training. God, as He was then and still is now, is raising up people who are willing to teach people how to truly live for God and to be used in some way in the expansion of the kingdom of God.

Paul, being the man that he was, had the heart and mind of God. Paul was ready and willing to take a stand against any incorrect ways of teaching Christians the proper ways of living for God. When you are ready and willing to truly become spiritual in God, you will take a stance against internal things that fight against this change in your life.

> *For the flesh lusts against the Spirit, and the Spirit against the flesh: and these are contrary the one to the other: so that ye cannot do the things that ye would. - Galatians 5:17*

The flesh also represents our Adamic nature, which is that part of us that glories in doing wrong. This part of us will fight against anything God requires us to do. So where does this leave us? It leaves us in a spiritual battle with the Holy Spirit working in us to help us make the right decision.

Without spending time building up our spiritual walk in Christ, guess who will win the battle of the mind every time? You have guessed right, the flesh!

At the Discipleship Center (DC), we teach people the importance of understanding who they are in God. It is so important that you understand this. When you know who you are and what you are capable of doing, nothing can stop you from accomplishing your goals. You are not caught in the middle of the road like a deer in front of an automobile, but instead you understand what is going on and you know how to handle the situation.

When becoming spiritual, understand that various tests will come. Do not be surprised or shocked when they come.

> *Beloved think it not strange concerning the fiery trial which is to try you, as though some strange thing happened unto you. - 1 Peter 4:12-17*

In maintaining daily spirituality, you are learning how to recognize what is happening to you. The flesh and the enemy are always up to something to prevent you from maturing spiritually in the manner that you should. Do not let these fiery trials get the best of you or trample on your nerves.

If you fail the test as a new born Christian, or perhaps even a seasoned Christian who is in the process of being healed and restored in their mind, just know that it is not the end of your walk with God and not too late to be restored, healed and delivered.

Tests are not allowed by God in any way to destroy who we are in God, but they are designed to mold and make us into who we are to be in God. Some failures are expected because we are not perfect beings. God is the only One who is perfect. We are just striving to be perfected in how we live for God.

We are all going through a process of change with a goal of receiving the full measure of our salvation at the return of Christ. So when a mistake is made, all you have to do is say Lord I am sorry, and prepare yourself for the next test to come.

Paul's intent in the New Covenant was to educate the saints to understand that although the laws of Moses were given for men to obey, these laws could not do what the Holy Spirit was able to do. The law did not give people supernatural power nor the ability to control how we live from day to day.

We do not want to be found guilty of being a long time member of the body of Christ and having walked in the flesh 100% of the time. If we are guilty of this, just know that God has given you a way out by truly becoming spiritual under apostolic teachings. If you are not willing to know God in a broader way versus how you were taught to know God through tradition and religious teachings, you may find it very difficult to believe that certain things can change.

Apostolic teachings can provide answers to the believer's prayer. It is up to the individual to consider, believe and accept what is being spoken of through apostolic teaching, instead of being opposed to what they may be hearing for the first time.

As you are becoming spiritual in God, initially your flesh, your soulish or lower nature, will communicate to your mind that this is NOT the right thing to do. This nature will tell you this is too much work, you do not have time for this, you have other things to do, and as a matter of fact, other things WILL come to your mind to take you away from spending time with God.

Religious people will not know their lower nature is working against the Godly work the Holy Spirit is birthing inside of them. They will automatically reject anything new, without thoroughly thinking it through.

The lower nature, or the flesh, contains a very convincing, manipulative, vindictive, occultist and cunning spirit that wants complete ownership of your mind. Just think about this for a moment as I attempt to give you an example. In your mind on Monday, you plan to spend time with God on Wednesday, which is your day off. So many other things will come up starting Tuesday that spill over into the time you planned to spend with God on Wednesday. Before you know it, the day has ended, there is still some energy left in you, and when you do think of just praying to God, all of a sudden a huge yawn comes out of nowhere. In this case, the lower nature has already sent a signal up to the mind telling you it is time for bed now.

I find then a law, that, when I would do good, evil is present with me. - Romans 7:21

> *For the flesh lusteth against the Spirit, and the Spirit against the flesh: and these are contrary the one to the other: so that ye cannot do the things that ye would. - Galatians 5:17*

In the spirit realm, the enemy uses tactics like this through our flesh to stop us from growing in God, so you cannot do the things that you would. The example above comes through apostolic teachings. Paul was apostolic and carried apostolic teachings with him everywhere he preached.

The Jews for the most part never welcomed and accepted the teachings of Paul. So while Paul and his followers were traveling to Macedonia, something unusual happened to them which caused them some delays in getting there. Titus and the saints did not understand why Paul had not arrived yet, but a virus of some sort broke out in Asia that caused them to feel sick unto death.

> *For we would not, brethren, have you ignorant of our trouble which came to us in Asia, that we were pressed out of measure, above strength, insomuch that we despaired even of life. But we had the sentence of death in ourselves, that we should not trust in ourselves, but in God which raise the dead. - 2 Corinthians 1:8-9*

This virus was not an ordinary virus that just so happened to appear in the city, but it was there as a result of what was about to come into that area. When apostolic leaders show up, the spirit of change comes along with them. Satan does not like change and will do whatever he can to prevent change from coming. Apostles who bring apostolic teachings and prophets who release strong edifications will bring immediate change into people's lives, environments, atmospheres, stratospheres and hemispheres. Because of this, opposition will come on every hand to stop apostolic teachings and works from coming forth.

Apostolic teachings are released from five-fold teams being apostles, prophets, evangelists, pastors and teachers. Believe it or not, these callings reside in people who don't know it because of denominations they have grown accustomed to.

These Jewish teachers believed in God and strongly trusted in themselves for what they believed to be true. There are a lot of people who are in God's house who feel the same way. To be honest, it is really not them who are kicking against new apostolic movements; it is spirits of tradition and religion that have a grip on them.

These spirits are hindering them from accepting anything new outside of what they were programmed to know before. This is also considered a stronghold. Apostolic anointings are designed to remove and to destroy this thinking from people and places setting the stage for change.

As you are becoming spiritual, when apostolic teachings and works come, you must embrace it with wide open arms. This is the key to your deliverance and in fulfilling the purpose God has for your life. In your mind, you must understand the tasks that God had given to the apostles who have been commissioned to establish the work. This understanding will come from knowing the basics of the Scriptures beginning with Acts of the Apostles.

God has a mandate that must be fulfilled in your life. That mandate will not be fulfilled by hanging on to religious theology and traditions of men. Paul knew that he could not allow this sickness in his flesh to cause him to think anything different. He knew this was a demonic attack because it prevented him from opening his mouth to release apostolic teachings to the saints.

When you begin your journey of becoming spiritual, understand that unexpected things may show up to prevent your transformation. Understand they are all sent from the enemy to stop it from happening. Satan will do whatever he can to stop people from truly becoming spiritual in God. He will work through other viral spirits such as manipulation, control, fear and familiar spirits from others to convince you to stop the progress.

The challenge that a new Christian faces when they make a decision to live for God is building themselves up in this most holy faith. People are challenged with hearing the truth of God's Word. Their emotions are challenged; their intellect is challenged because people assume that they know more about building a relationship with God without having the Spirit of God in them.

The key to becoming spiritual is to not trust in ourselves in terms of what we may know about God through religion, but rather trust in God through relationship. Becoming Spiritual is all about spiritual relationship building.

This is why Jesus said we must be born again, not from another natural birth, but a spiritual birth.

> *But ye, beloved, building up yourselves on your most holy faith, praying in the Holy Ghost, Keep yourselves in the love of God, looking for the mercy of our Lord Jesus Christ unto eternal life.*
> *- Jude 1:20-21*

We must have no dependence in our flesh, especially when we know one moment things are going well, we are focused on what God is doing in us and on what we are to do for Him, and then all of a sudden strange things begin to happen just to take our attention off what God is doing in our lives. We go about on any given day, strong in the Lord and in the power of His might, alert, sharp and on top of everything. The Lord tells us pray, next thing we know, all of a sudden we get sleepy. That is the flesh trying to get us to not pray.

Who do we trust in this case? The flesh or the Lord? We trust in the Lord and pray anyway. We make a decision to fast, and the next thing we know, a sickness comes on us, which is the flesh trying to get us to not fast.

In other cases, the devil throws things into our lives just to distract us, now our focus is off what the Lord is telling us and we are now concentrating on what just happened. Who do we trust in this case? The flesh or the Lord? We trust in the Lord and fast anyhow.

Always remember that there is a danger of trusting in your own knowledge. There is a danger of rejecting apostolic knowledge. Becoming spiritual protects you from this mental harm.

Calvin B. Collins, Sr.

Chapter 5-Letting the Holy Spirit Lead You

For as many as are led by the Spirit of God, they are the sons of God. - Romans 8:14

Truly spiritual people are led by the Spirit of God in all that they do. They learn to rely on the Holy Spirit by tearing down their old patterns and schemas and building new ones. They learn to understand the importance of Scripture. They learn to not rely on the first thought in doing things. They understand the course of this world has taught them to think this way.

God identifies His sons and daughters by how they are living for Him. God proudly says these people are a part of Me. They have My attributes and My name is written in them.

God does wish not to have disobedient sons and daughters, however in this world, there are many because they have not been taught properly how to be led by the Holy Spirit.

In the last chapter, the Lord gave us insight concerning some newly converted Christians who were trying to live based on this new lifestyle that Paul preached, while still caught up in ways of living based on the laws of Moses that were taught by Jewish teachers. This is still common today. There are many churches today filled with people who are still living two lives. Their old ways of seeing, hearing and understanding things still exist, while claiming to be spirit led people.

New Testament Jewish teachers brought conflict to the body of Christ in terms of what Christians can or cannot do. This led new Christians to believe they could live and do anything they wanted to do and still be identified as a Christian. This is still popular in the 21st century church today.

> *Therefore if any man be in Christ, he is a new creature: old things are passed away; behold, all things are become new. - 2 Corinthians 5:17*

Paul said that if any man be in Christ, meaning if any man or woman has accepted the Lord into their hearts and understand the importance of having the Holy Spirit living in them, they are expected to become new people.

When a person receives salvation and the Holy Spirit, their lives are supposed to change. God never intended that people receive salvation, and some also receiving the Holy Spirit, and remain on the same level of understanding of God for years. The newness or change that God brings to people does not occur automatically. Specific steps are to be given by spirit led pastors that must be followed in order for the conversion to progress properly.

> *See if there be any wicked way in me, and lead me in the way everlasting. - Psalm 139:24*

The word wicked in the above Scripture has to do with pain, hurt, toil, sorrow, labor, hardship and offences that make people respond differently towards things, themselves and other people. Each person may handle them different. What they experience can affect what they do and say. It will affect what other people think about them because of their actions.

When proper teaching and understanding of God and the Holy Spirit are absent from the mind of the Christian, their old ways of living becomes more harden. This flaw is the root cause of why people do not have a real relationship with the Lord.

Today the old behaviors are not passing away as they should. People are holding on to these ways. Christians are holding on to these ways. Many do not know they need to change their ways. They do not want to let them go because it has been a part of their lives for many years. To change this mindset, God releases a new approach and a new grace to understand Him through His Holy Spirit. The Holy Spirit is here to teach us how to live in this world and how to enjoy the many benefits of the Kingdom of God. This is the newness that all mankind can expect if accepted through salvation and the Holy Spirit.

When you are becoming spiritual in God correctly, you benefit from new ways, new standards, new outlooks, new views and new courses of life to live by. God made this available for all people regardless of their ethnicity, race, color or creed. You can know God on a much deeper personal level through this new way. This way is not taught by man's ability, but only by the Holy Spirit.

True spiritual leaders in the body of Christ will consistently point people back to God to confirm how He wants them to live. True spiritual leaders lead by example in all honesty and a pure conscience.

When people are positioned to be led of God, their lives will change in every aspect. They will change mentally, physically, psychologically, emotionally and socially. They will look back at their old ways of living, compare them to how the Spirit of God has now taught them to live and say to themselves "I should have lived this way from the beginning."

True spiritual leaders will bring to people great understanding of things. There are root causes for every issue that people have. True spiritual leaders can and will provide spiritual understanding for these root causes. Pastors who are not prepared to give spiritual understanding for why things continue to happen in a person's life can leave the people they lead exposed to great danger. People who are not wise and strong enough in spirit to go after the answers themselves are adding more danger to themselves. There are many spiritual reasons for each issue a person has.

When a person is led by a man or woman who perpetrates as if they are living for God and that person's life has not changed, it is possible that this person is under some type of spiritually rooted control.

It is evident that we live in a world that can cause us to change some behaviors. We are born and shaped with wrong ways of living, thinking, hearing and understanding. Most Christians do not know this. They automatically assume that once you become a Christian, things automatically change within themselves. This is 100% false.

Transformation begins with you making the transition, not the pastor. The pastor's role is to point you in the direction of change. You are to make it happen. This is why Paul said for us to be transformed by the renewing of our mind.

And be not conformed to this world: but be ye transformed by the renewing of your mind, that ye

> *may prove what is that good, and acceptable, and perfect, will of God.* - Romans 12:2

This transformation is called the wheel of life. It's up to us to make decisions as to where the dial stops. The renewing of the mind is the most avoided part of this Scripture.

The word mind in the Greek gives us the word *neous* or *psyche*, which means the intellect thought, the understanding.

To become spiritual, Dennis R. Jacobs said you must renew, renovate, and reform with repetitiveness your thought patterns, feelings, will, understanding and even your intellect. You cannot fully please God if you are not being challenged to constantly learn something new or re-learn something.

All things and every event that takes place in our lives happen for a reason. Our lives are wrapped around events that will happen in seasons and times. Learning how to deal with these events has been the challenge for many people, especially when living in a world where there are so many options in dealing with events.

What you need to know and understand as a Christian is that God is in control over everything that happens. God sends good things our way and He allows the bad things to come. It is all a part of the process of becoming spiritual. Keep in mind that everyone's process is NOT the same.

If you do not educate yourself in spiritual things and implement new things into your spirit in an uncompromising way, your spiritual growth will be stagnate. You will remain a carnal Christian with carnal understanding. You must let God lead you through this journey with obedience and humility.

One of the greatest frustrations in the kingdom of God is to see people who are stuck in religion, meaning they do not want to let go of the old and grab a hold of something new. They will not humble themselves. They have grown accustomed to living the same lack luster and feel good about it.

God expects every Christian to move forward and learn more about Him and not stay on the same level of just knowing about God. Education is the key to going from glory to glory. Other books have been written to support what is found in Scripture, whereby God continues to give revelation regarding that which is written in His Word. You must read other spiritual books that connects with how God wants to renew your mind. This is when prophecy comes in to reveal more truth about God and His will or choices for mankind.

> *We have also a more sure word of prophecy;*
> *whereunto ye do well that ye take heed, as unto a*
> *light that shineth in a dark place, until the day*
> *dawn, and the day star arise in your hearts.*
> *- 2 Peter 1:19*

When you are led by the Holy Spirit, you will do well. The key is taking heed to the light. Jesus is the light of the world. In his triune state, the Holy Spirit is that Light. This light reveals to people the essence of God. This light also reveals the truth about things people do not understand, whether natural or spiritual. Nothing is hidden once this light shines. The truth will come forth. This light brings clear understanding of things into the dark hearts and minds of Christians who are not spirit filled. The believer will experience ongoing revelations about God that does not end when they take heed to what the Spirit is saying.

When people are having difficult times seeing their way, light is missing. People have to be taught how to use that Light. They have to keep the fire of God burning in their life and depend on that Light to make it. They have to trust that Light. Most importantly, they have to believe that same Light shines through people such as their pastors. Failure to see this true Light in pastors will yield them negative results in their personal growth in God. This is because they have not learned to see and accept that God is speaking directly to them from their pastors.

Darkness that is present in the lives of people prevents them from following the light. They will see true pastors as normal people, not true spiritual people. Darkness prevents them from believing God is in the pastors therefore they are skeptical in following their directions. If you are a part of a ministry were apostolic teachings is present, and you are aware of cynical Christians, they are this way because some form of darkness still resides in them. This is why deliverance ministry is needed in places of worship.

A person can be a part of a ministry for years and still be in the dark with no real directions. Darkness prevents people from connecting to the right people. The right people can be literally in front of them with answers to their problems. The Holy Spirit's guidance gives everlasting light. It shines every day and every night to give us perfect direction.

When salvation came into the world through Christ, God at that time gave all people light to shine in their lives. This Light made it possible for people to escape from a torn apart life. God made a way for people to be free from mental bondage and torment.

Change only comes by people actively doing something. When you are led by the Holy Spirit, you are actively doing something to build yourself up in the knowledge of God. When the flesh is leading you, take notice that very little time is spent in your personal development in the things of God. This is because by fallen nature, people tend to believe they know how to grow in the knowledge of God with what knowledge that may already have.

> *Every way of a man is right in his own eyes: but the LORD pondereth the hearts. - Proverbs 21:2*

Darkness in the mind causes people to run away from new things and to not spend quality time with God. Darkness causes people to be comfortable living in ways that seems right in their own eyes. Depending on the Holy Spirit to lead them does not become a priority. You must make this a high priority to become spiritual, otherwise you will remain carnal in your thinking while loving God.

Carnal minded people are drawn to carnal things that pleases the flesh. Carnal people would rather not understand real issues, but view them as the norm.

The good part about having relationship with God is that we can understand the root cause of the things we encounter, such as what made me say those words, why did I feel that way, why do I do certain things repeatedly and who else in my family is dealing with these same issues.

The Holy Spirit will always question your motives when you are spirit led. The Holy Spirit will inform us if our motives are bad. Conviction will come by the Holy Spirit as He leads us. Conviction is of the Holy Spirit.

Condemnation, guilt and shame are all emotional feelings that people have when they do fleshly things.

When conviction comes, correction comes with it, which is by the Holy Spirit. This is why our motives must be checked often.

God's true pastors will consistently challenge their motives to make sure they are up to par with God, as well as challenging the motives of the people they teach. If the Christian's life is not changing for the good day to day, that person should check their motives as well as their pastor's motives.

> *For the time will come when they will not endure sound doctrine; but after their own lusts shall they heap to themselves teachers, having itching ears.*
> *- 2 Timothy 4:3.*

We live in times now where Christians are rejecting the truth of God's word, especially those who have been saved for a long period of time. They think they are full of knowledge having been taught through tradition and religion. These spirits are operating in the land and will not allow them to grab hold to apostolic teachings.

Many will not accept change because they do not know how. Once again they are in need of a deliverance ministry. Others will pretend to know how, but have no real intentions of changing due to selfish, traditional, and religious reasons.

They would rather stick to things they have learned in the past years than to embrace something new. They will look for and strongly desire other pastors and motivational speakers who will not challenge them to turn away from their traditional-religious teachings.

What you have read thus far are good examples of a Christian who is not led by the Spirit, but by the flesh. God's primary agenda for people was to receive the Holy Ghost so that we can become spiritually minded Christians being led by God.

If Jesus was not led by God while in a fleshly body, then we can imagine what people would have had to say about the lifestyle He lived on Earth. Those who were looking for a way out would have found it difficult to follow Him as an example.

Jesus was led by God 100% of His time on Earth. He gave us examples on how to let God lead us. Because of this, He did things right, made the right statements and responded accordingly in all things.

> *Then answered Jesus and said unto them, Verily, verily, I say unto you, The Son can do nothing of himself, but what he seeth the Father do: for what things soever he doeth, these also doeth the Son likewise. - John 5:19*

Jesus knew what to say and what not to say. He was always careful with His words and through God's discernment, He got it right each time. People could not find fault in Jesus because He demonstrated to the entire world how to be spiritual and how not to live in the flesh. With proper teaching by true pastors, you can be taught these things. When the flesh is in control, it has a major impact on the life of a Christian. Fleshly desires will slow down spiritual maturity.

If you are becoming spiritual, you must deny your flesh and accept what God is giving you to do, hear, and understand. A spiritually minded man or woman embraces Biblical truth. They understand there are areas in people that God wishes to correct. They follow up with immediate action plans. You can expect great results when you are letting the Holy Spirit lead you.

Chapter 6-Things You Must Do

Those things, which ye have both learned, and received, and heard, and seen in me, do: and the God of peace shall be with you. - Philippians 4:9

Apostles, prophets, pastors, teachers and evangelists cannot make you spiritual. They can lay hands on you and or give you words of prophecy, and this five-fold team can spiritually activate gifts and abilities in you, but it will be up to you to utilize what is given to become spiritual. Again, you will have to make this happen. Your lifestyle has to change in terms of how you think, see and understand. You will have to work in order to become spiritual.

As a concerned Pastor, the task I have is to bring God's people back into having a spiritual relationship with God. In doing so, there are things that God holds the people responsible for in order to bring this change back. First and foremost, every victory over the enemy will depend on knowledge and your obedience to spiritual growth.

Every accomplishment will depend on how much God is allowed to work His will in you. Your natural and spiritual life is in your own hands. What you do with the both of them matters to God. The ability to choose whether to allow or to disallow the Holy Spirit to operate in you is placed into your own hands. **You must submit your will to God.**

> *Behold, I set before you this day a blessing and a curse; A blessing, if ye obey the commandments of the LORD your God, which I command you this day, and a curse, if ye will not obey the commandments of the LORD your God, but turn aside out of the way which I command you this day, to go after other gods, which ye have not known.*
> *- Deuteronomy 11:26-28*

The word curse here in the Hebrew gives us the word *Qow-Lal*, which means to be slighted, to come short of something, to have things taken away, not come your way or to take a risk of not having THE blessing that God has for you. These types of curses come because people choose to not obey God's commandments because of ignorance.

Hence the reason why a person can believe in God, still struggle, and not know how to get out of this cursed state. This explains why things do not go well when they try. It is the same cursed state that happens to a person when they hold back the tithes and offerings spoken of in Malachi. Understand that this curse state does not mean you will go through life and nothing will go right, it only means that individuals will come short of things. Ever heard the saying a day late and a dollar short?

Obeying God's commandments is more than just coming to the place of worship. It involves a series of changes in your home life as well. **You must live a lifestyle of worship**. Your journey into having a blessed spiritual life starts at home. You are the shepherd over your soul at home, while driving, while walking, while at work and even around family and friends.

You are responsible for governing over your mind, the state of your spiritual body, and your spirit. It is your responsibility to watch over yourself to ensure you are growing and maturing in the Lord properly.

> *Watch ye therefore, and pray always, that ye may be accounted worthy to escape all these things that shall come to pass, and to stand before the Son of man. - Luke 21:36*

You have to watch over yourself now more than ever to ensure the course of this world, which is governed by the prince of the power of the air, has not persuaded you to not keeping a close tab on building your relationship with God.

Remember, the enemy called satan is very cunning and subtle. The enemy will have you so busy doing other things on a daily basis that you will not have time to grow in the knowledge of Jesus Christ. You will not have time to even think about spending quality time with God until it is so late in the evening and it's time to go to sleep. The enemy will very smoothly convince Spirit-Filled believers to get it done tomorrow only to find themselves with more things to do than spending time with God. **You must take heed to this alarm in your life and come to the conclusion that I am through living to please myself, but instead, fully committed to pleasing God.**

When people first accept Jesus as their Lord and Savior, someone has to teach them the other side of Christianity. This side is mostly omitted and overlooked because of the course of this world. I call it the system at work. Understand that your current ways of seeing, hearing and understanding are supposed to change when you receive salvation and are baptized with the Holy Spirit. If you are claiming salvation and claim to be spirit filled, but how you see, hear, and understand things have not changed for many years, accept the fact that something has gone wrong with your walk in the Lord. Something is missing and you must question yourself asking, "What has gone wrong?"

First begin with you. Have you grown in terms of understanding why you received salvation? Understand that salvation just prevents you from going to hell. It does not stop you from experiencing or living a hard life, which some liken to a hell.

People get saved for many reasons. The main reason should have been to live for God.

Many are looking to get back to having a spiritual life with God as it was in the garden prior to the fall of man and they do not know it. They receive salvation to save their marriage, to save a relationship from crumbling or to escape from some type of trouble. These are just some reasons people give.

Christians who are leading people to Christ should be pointing them back to living a holy life. Their current patterns of life should come to a halt. They are to be given action plans to follow every week by their pastors who are led by the Spirit to build them up in God every day by the Holy Spirit on a personal level.

> *Behold, I was shapen in iniquity; and in sin did my mother conceive me. - Psalm 51:5*

David said we were all born and shapen in iniquity and in sin did my mother conceive me. Iniquity and sin in the proper context has to do with wrongful ways of responding, doing, seeing, hearing, and understanding things.

When people are born into this world, if their parents were not taught properly how to live the Christian life, that child is born and brought into this world with a mindset that is already conformed to how the world would handle things. Let's say now that child receives salvation. More than likely, that child will continue to do things the way mom and dad did things and can essentially repeat the same mistakes they have if their minds do not conform to the mind of Christ. That child, or now adult, will continue down this path even after becoming a Christian, not understanding that there are things they must change themselves in order to become spiritual.

Becoming spiritual does not happen automatically. You cannot make a wish for this and do nothing for it to come to pass. If you say you will wait for God to mold and make you, you will be waiting your entire life. God will not do this for you, without your cooperation.

> *Wherefore, my beloved, as ye have always obeyed, not as in my presence only, but now much more in my absence, work out your own salvation with fear and trembling. - Philippians 2:12*

This is NOT an automatic change over. If you are still fussing, cursing, swearing, living unholy, dealing with hurt, pain, fear of your life or fear of others, full of condemnation, guilt or shame, and hiding personal issues about yourself, your family or loved ones, know that you have been trained by the course of this world to fool yourself into thinking you are just fine and that things will get better by and by. Something has hindered your growth in God. The finger pointing starts with you and how satan has convinced you to not spend time with God on a personal level. The next finger could be who you may have selected to be your pastor.

Remember, you are supposed to be growing in the knowledge of God. Your life is supposed to change. If you are not changing, examine yourself first. You must allow the Holy Spirit to transform how you see, hear and understand things.

The Holy Spirit wants to switch you over from a worldly way of doing things to a spiritual way of doing things. This is your renewal of the mind process. Renewal is simply gaining additional knowledge. Education is the key. When proper education comes, action plans come with it. Every message you hear from the preacher, you should develop an action implementing what was spoken into your life.

And be not conformed to this world: but be ye transformed by the renewing of your mind, that ye may prove what is that good, and acceptable, and perfect, will of God. - Romans 12:2

Over the years, I have witnessed many times the saints at Healing and Restoration Discipleship Center (HRDC) undergoing personal deliverances that began at home. They have learned to put action plans together through the leading of the Holy Spirit as they are hearing the Word of God coming forth. They are not waiting to have hands laid on them by the pastors. Although there are times when this is required, because of proper education, they understand they too have the power in them to set themselves free.

We are receiving testimony after testimony of such great deliverances including generational curses and yokes being destroyed in their lives. The Holy Spirit will lead and guide you into all truths through insight and revelation.

Read the Bible as well as other good books that feed you with knowledge. God did not stop speaking after the Bible was written. People are still writing His heart and mind in other books such as this one.

Listening to sermons and not taking the time to understand what you are listening to is a sure way of keeping you in the dark concerning things. What you think you know about life and in making decisions has to be renewed, understood, accepted and done the way Christ would have it to be done.

You should not see things the way you would normally see them. You should not receive and understand the way you would normally do. Everything has to change so you can begin to flow through spiritual insight and understanding. You have to make this happen through the guidance of the Holy Spirit. The purpose for our Lord sending us the Holy Spirit is for us to allow the Holy Ghost to teach us how to live life, carry out our purpose and to give us clarity of His Word.

> *When I call to remembrance the unfeigned faith that is in thee, which dwelt first in thy grandmother Lois, and thy mother Eunice; and I am persuaded that in thee also. - 2 Timothy 1:5*

Paul gave Timothy, whose name means "honoring God", great encouragement as he obeyed the commandments of God. Paul was a type of Holy Spirit for young Timothy, who was learning how to depend on the Holy Spirit. As Paul brings things back to Timothy's remembrance, the Holy Spirit will also bring things back to your remembrance.

> *But the Comforter, which is the Holy Ghost, whom the Father will send in my name, he shall teach you all things, and bring all things to your remembrance, whatsoever I have said unto you. - John 14:26*

The Holy Spirit speaks to us in the same manner in words easily understood.

Timothy was an honest young man who believed in fairness. He developed good integrity and people highly respected him. Unknown to Timothy, his maturation process was preparing him for an assignment. His assignment was to preach the truth of God's Word to a nation of teachers, who were not about our Lord's business.

People should get saved to honor God in all that they do, and not to escape from life's trouble. When people are not taught properly how to live as a Christian, they continue to do things that does not bring honor to God.

The Pastor's role is to confirm the gifts in people and to teach them how to walk in them. You should have a plan for personal development in place and stick to it. Ongoing spiritual warfare will decrease because you are building yourself up in God. The enemy will back up, but only for a season.

> *Those by the way side are they that hear; then cometh the devil, and taketh away the word out of*

their hearts, lest they should believe and be saved. - Luke 8:12

When people are not aware of the system that is at work, the demonic forces in the air will cause God's plan to not reach the mind of the Christian. They will simply forget the plan that was just given to them because no one explained anything about spiritual warfare to them.

You must understand that God has an assignment for you. In Paul's spirit, he knew the Lord was ready to use him. Timothy lacked confidence in himself and allowed fear to grip his heart at times. Timothy was not afraid of the Lord using him. He was more concerned with who he had to confront, which were corrupt teachers that were enslaving, stunning and preventing the growth of God's people.

Wherefore I put thee in remembrance that thou stir up the gift of God, which is in thee by the putting on of my hands. - 2 Timothy 1:6

Every person born in this world has spiritual gifts placed in them by God. I believe God left no one behind in terms of placing them to work somewhere in the kingdom of God. God said we were predetermined, ordained and predestined for these gifts to arise. Someone has to already know this prior to birth; someone has to cater to this after birth, otherwise the gifts will lie dormant, their minds will never be transformed from evil to good. As a result, progress in kingdom expansion becomes stagnant.

You must exercise the spiritual gift or gifts and callings that you have been given. The Holy Spirit will lead you to the right spiritual place and people in order for this confirmation to take place.

Renewed knowledge and educational facts are critical for building salvation and becoming spiritual.

True pastors bring deliverance to people as well as identify, affirm and help cultivate gifts in them to help others. They do not keep gifted people to themselves for personal gain. Timothy's gift was a prophetic gift which was to hear the heart and mind of God and respond.

His mission was to bring proper government to the churches so that lives could be changed for the better. You cannot allow the spirit of fear to operate in you.

For God hath not given us the spirit of fear; but of power, and of love, and of a sound mind.
- 2 Timothy 1:7

God wants to establish His government in you. People need to hear the voice of God coming from your mouth. You can speak prophetically also. To speak a prophetic word is to simply hear the voice of God and respond accordingly. God is all about change.

The world was created through a process and so are Christians who are Holy Ghost filled. You must not be afraid of change. You have to be strong. You have to stand firm. You have to be fully confident in your relationship with the Lord.

Religious people will challenge your approach of becoming spiritual. The spirits in them will tell you that your approach to becoming spiritual is not required, you should not have to do all of that and you are wasting your time. Certain demonic spirits control what people think and do.

Do not be afraid of doing better, embrace it. You MUST have confidence in the Lord that the Holy Spirit is going to reveal to you something new and exciting. When this happens, understand you are not the only person who is feeling this or receiving the new found enlightenment. You are not going crazy and there are others in the world who feel the same way. If you are a preacher, your preaching will change.

Embrace and allow God to do in you what He desires to do. You must desire to do better. Don't be satisfied on the current level you are on in the Lord. It is not where you should stay at. God has more to reveal to you.

You do not have to be an apostle, pastor, prophet, evangelist, bishop, superintendent to be spiritual. It is not about us as individuals trying to get ahead, it is about us allowing God's will to work in us. God desires all people of all ages to be spiritual in Him. Finally, you must understand, obey and know what the will of God is for your life.

They which live should not henceforth live unto themselves, but unto him which died for them, and rose again. - 2 Corinthians 5:15(b)

The above Scripture describes the will of God for your life. You were not born in this world to live for yourself to fulfill your own purposes. God brought you in this world to live for Him and to fulfill His purposes. Becoming spiritual brings to life the gifts in you. You regain spiritual strength in the Lord to fight off the temptations of the world.

True spiritual strength comes from deliverance ministries. You need to be a part of a deliverance ministry in order to effectively become spiritual. Until then, your ability to see, hear, and understand things will remain the same. God has given us the power to overcome obstacles and a deliverance ministry can teach you how to overcome these things.

A deliverance ministry is defined as a designated place that offers Christians an outlet to receive personal deliverance, instructions and guidance. This type of ministry usually refers to as being delivered from demonic influences and spirits disrupting the individual's life.

Most demonic influences come from generational and ancestral curses that have invaded families through disobedience to God. Many are avoidable and controllable. They can be cast down and destroyed. With proper spiritual guidance, you can believe and obey the voice of the Holy Spirit that is now operating in you to help you overcome and win these battles. These are just a few things that you must do.

Chapter 7-Identifying Vital Signs

And the Spirit of the LORD will come upon thee, and thou shalt prophesy with them, and shalt be turned into another man. And let it be, when these signs are come unto thee, that thou do as occasion serve thee; for God is with thee. - 1 Samuel 10:6-7

As you desire to become spiritual, the Spirit of the Lord will rest upon you. You will begin to speak the truth of who God is and His will for mankind. This truth about God being revealed is prophesy.

As you are learning how to be spiritual, you are becoming someone new. The changes in your life will happen because God is with you. As a people, coming to a place of worship "aka church" was never designed to be a waste of time or to simply be a place to just go to have a good time.

Those who have put into practice the things that they have heard from the pastors at the Discipleship Center (DC) are happy to see changes in their lives. I thank God for being in a position of identifying wrong and to have a platform and opportunity to explain and teach people how to make things right.

When you learn to identify error in you, always implement an action plan to deal with the symptom. You are actually identifying the vital signs of your spiritual growth. The word vital means the essential parts or elements of something. The Holy Spirit is essential for every believer to have.

The elements of the Holy Spirit are important to have working inside of us as people. What and how you say and do things to build yourself up in God are important vital signs. If you are not watching what you say and do, you can hinder the growth in yourself and others in their walk with God.

You must work hard by putting to death or denying the things that you desire more than understanding your role and position within the kingdom of God. What your eyes want in the natural can be distractions. They are in place to draw you away from building yourself up in God if you are not careful. Your position is to not get caught up in wanting the things of this natural world. You are to desire the spiritual things more.

> *As it is written, Eye hath not seen, nor ear heard, neither have entered into the heart of man, the things which God hath prepared for them that love him. - 1 Corinthians 2:9*

There are things that God wants to reveal to every Christian who is serious about having a relationship with the Lord. Many people choose however to forfeit the promise that God made to them. Christian leaders play a vital role in helping their followers reach this point in their walk with God. There has to be a consistency in the messages that are relayed from Christian leaders in terms of instruction and their followers must apply these principles daily in order to bring the vision to past.

Paul talked about us first being partakers of the fruit of the Spirit in Galatians 5, which are vital signs of one having the Holy Spirit actively working in them. God has given my wife Kimberly great teaching ability in expounding on these vital signs. They are all good indications of a Christian who is learning to become spiritual. When Paul commented on these vital signs, he did not have just Timothy in mind in terms of becoming spiritual, he was speaking about the maturation of every Christian that wants to become spiritual.

God created these vital signs for the elect's sake, to develop and fully equip those who are willing and ready to change into becoming better people and real Christians in the eyes of God. When a person receives the Holy Spirit, at some point in their relationship with the Lord they are to show spiritual vital signs. These vital signs come from one fruit that has different parts. We cannot have one without the other. We need them all. They all belong to the Holy Spirit and are to be alive and manifest in all that we do.

The word manifest simply means to display or show that something is seen or identified by the visual senses of a person. Every Christian MUST be properly taught how to demonstrate these signs.

> *But the fruit of the Spirit is love, joy, peace,*
> *longsuffering, gentleness, goodness, faith,*
> *meekness, temperance: against such there is no law.*
> *- Galatians 5:22-23*

Knowing how to love is the first part of the one fruit that every Christian should learn to produce rather quickly. For some people, it will require much deliverance to acquire. Love in this case has to do with the ability of respecting and understanding God and knowing what drives people to do the things they do.

If you know of someone who does evil or bad all the time, becoming spiritual will teach you to continue to love that person and also to understand that it is not that person doing the evil or that they have bad intentions. You understand that person needs deliverance and it is really not them doing the devilish work. So you still love them. When you have this love operating in you, you will understand that people are not completely to blame for their careless actions, but again, some type of evil spirit is the root cause of why they do the things they do. You learn to look past the person and look directly at the spirit that is driving them to do the wrong that they do.

For every wrong action that a person does, it is because they were programmed or taught to do them prior to receiving Jesus Christ. This is caused by demonic influence and or by demonic air assaults.

> *Wherein in time past ye walked according to the course of this world, according to the prince of the power of the air, the spirit that now worketh in the children of disobedience. - Ephesians 2:2*

Ever wonder where some thoughts, ideas or suggestions come from all of a sudden? Ever plan to do something for God and then all of a sudden you find yourself doing something else instead? Notice that when you purpose in your heart to pray and spend time reading or studying, you are reminded of other important tasks that must be done at the same time. Notice how they will take higher priority over what you need to do in order to grow by spending time with God. These are aerial assaults sent from satan to block your progress in growing spiritually.

The proper way to advance spiritually is when you receive salvation and the Holy Ghost, you are to learn about these types of attacks and how to fight to keep them from being effective in your life. The Holy Spirit and spiritual guidance helps to orchestrate these actions. If people refuse to understand this or refuse to believe this to be true, they will continue to treat other people in a non-loving manner assuming they are always right.

> *For we wrestle not against flesh and blood, but*
> *against principalities, against powers, against the*
> *rulers of the darkness of this world, against*
> *spiritual wickedness in high places.*
> *- Ephesians 6:12*

Paul said for we wrestle not against flesh and blood, this is represented through people. If you are having altercations with a spouse, son, daughter, father, mother, love one, enemy or stranger, understand that it is not them that you are angry with, it is the spirit or spirits in them that you should be addressing. Our fight is not with people, but as Paul mentioned, our fight is with principalities, powers, rulers of the darkness of this world and spiritual wickedness in high places.

Christians are expected to learn how to identify which spirit is speaking out of the person. Once this has been accomplished, they are to learn how to properly deal with the spirit(s).

Principalities come from the Greek word *archer* which means beginning or origin of spirits. Principalities are also called second heaven rulers because they were found to be evil. God's kingdom or throne resides in the third heaven where there is no evil. Paul makes reference to a man being caught up in the third heaven in *2 Corinthians 12:2 – I knew a man in Christ above fourteen years ago, (whether in the body, I cannot tell; or whether out of the body, I cannot tell: God knoweth;) such an one caught up to the third heaven.*

These principalities are evil spirits that can only be fought in the spirit realm. God, His heavenly hosts and spiritual people operate from the third heaven. Ruling demonic spirits such as insecurity, inferiority, fear, anger, control, manipulation or frustration for example, all operate in the lives of people spiritually from the second heaven. The powers are spirits that affect people by using its delegated authority or powers from principalities.

The rulers of the darkness of this world are spirits responsible for preventing the truth from entering into the mind of believers. They are also responsible, by any means necessary, for hindering or preventing people from making spiritual connections with Christians who understand clearly Ephesians 6:12. And lastly, spiritual wickedness in high places are spirits responsible for perverting the mindsets of people. These spirits have rank. First in line are principalities, second are powers, third are rulers of darkness and then spiritual wickedness in high places.

In order to really become spiritual, you must believe and understand the principal of Ephesians 6:12. They all affect what we do as people and as Christians. These spiritual entities can and will operate through human beings. Their purpose is to prevent your God created personality from coming forth. Without God's love actively working in you, you will fail multiple tests when living and working with people.

Demonstrating love can be natural for some people, while others may not know how to show or to have love for someone else. This example can also be done falsely by a person controlled by spirits described in Ephesians 6:12. These are vital signs of someone who has not learned how to properly discern what is controlling people.

Love is something everyone is born with. God placed this into every person's DNA. If no one is available to teach people how to love, they will be known as a cold hearted person. Some people come from families whose mothers and fathers did not know how to love them. So when people come into the knowledge of the truth through proper teaching and receive the Holy Spirit, the Holy Spirit will teach people how to flow in this love one to another. They will learn to know that it's not the person who is manifesting the hate, but that it's a spirit(s) that's preventing them from understanding what's causing them to say and do the evil things according to Ephesians 6:12.

For the kingdom of God is not meat and drink; but righteousness, and peace, and joy in the Holy Ghost. - Romans 14:17

The joy of the Holy Spirit is what causes us to have gladness and to rarely have or appear to have a dull moment. The peace of the Holy Spirit is what gives us a sense of security about ourselves in the Lord. We learn to not be overly concerned or worried about things. It will take much prayer, much laying on of the hands and much deliverance in order to prepare the minds of individuals to understand how not to be anxious.

No matter what goes on, the Holy Ghost gives us peace in our hearts. The longsuffering side of the Holy Spirit is what gives us the ability to be patient in all things. This is where trust is required.

If your mind is not made up with regards to living for God, you will continue to struggle due to a lack of patience. You will continue to live life the way it was before coming to Jesus Christ. God uses circumstances and situations to break people free from things. You may not know or understand why things happen to you, but God does because He has a plan.

> *I have seen the travail, which God hath given to the sons of men to be exercised in it. - Ecclesiastes 3:10*

Solomon lists twenty-eight categories of things that will transpire in every person's life. Each category has a list of things that is infinity.

God allows things to happen to develop us into becoming strong Christians. Longsuffering gives us the power to go through these processes. The Holy Spirit's gentle side gives us the ability to properly handle the situations that arise in our lives and especially with other people. It makes us into a well defined Christian with integrity.

The Holy Spirit's goodness gives us the ability to have a kind heart. It goes hand in hand with gentleness. This vital sign enables us to reach out and touch someone else in the right manner. On the other hand, cold hearted people could care less about others.

The Holy Spirit's faith gives us a spiritual faith to work with our natural faith that we demonstrated upon receiving salvation. This faith is what causes us to really believe God. This faith empowers us to have a stronger belief in God.

The Holy Spirit's meekness is what gives us the ability to have a calm temper. I call this the ability to chill out and not overreact towards things or not to become easily upset about things. Meekness also represents someone who is humble.

In order to become spiritual, it requires a great amount of humility. When God, through His infinite wisdom, places people in your life who are truly speaking the heart and mind of God for your life, you must have this humility. If you continue to see these people as ordinary people just like you, it will cause you to be a Christian full of pride, you will rebel against your spiritual leaders, and this will hinder your growth in the Lord. You must be willing to do and to accept what is being placed before you by your spiritual leaders.

Lastly, the Holy Spirit releases temperance, which gives us the ability to have self-control. You cannot allow your past experience or emotional outbursts to be in front of anything the Holy Spirit has commissioned to do in your life.

As your mind is being properly renewed, first by acceptance and then through knowledge, God will thrust out the past emotional statements that cause you to react when certain words, statements and situations are presented to you. This explains why before people have come into the knowledge of the truth, and they get angry nobody wants to be in the house with them. True deliverance and assistance by the Holy Spirit removes this uncontrollable nature away from us.

The Holy Spirit replaces this nature with a spiritual power called temperance. With this entity, you will learn how to respond properly thereby avoiding unnecessary altercations. Why? Because you have learned to understand it may not be the human individual you're wrestling with, it could very well be another spirit controlling them and their own words.

Man-made laws, ten-step programs, rehabs or boot camps can NOT implement these life changing attributes into the lives of people. Only the Holy Spirit can do this when properly understood and received. A person can have the Holy Spirit in them and never learn to live and obey what the Holy Spirit is giving them. For example, a person can accept Jesus as their Lord and Savior and receive the Holy Spirit. They are a member of the church for years, however the pastor may never expound on the benefits of having the Holy Spirit operating in your daily. Subsequently, they may not think to get this understanding on their own. Therefore, after years of being a Christian, the member lacks the understanding of how to allow the Holy Spirit to operate in them.

When God gets through with us, we will have become a completed work. Improper teaching has made many Christians an incomplete work. God wants you to have a clear view of who you are with the Holy Spirit living inside of you. You are in this world to represent the kingdom of God. By acknowledging within yourself that you have the right vital signs working in you with the Holy Spirit, you will have the ability to know, understand, and hear His Word better, as well as comprehend things better.

Chapter 8-Understanding Burdens

Take my yoke upon you, and learn of me; for I am meek and lowly in heart: and ye shall find rest unto your souls. For my yoke is easy, and my burden is light. - Matthew 11:30-31

What are burdens? Webster defines burden as something that is carried, such as a load. It is defined as a duty or responsibility. When defined in the Greek, it simply means to have obligations.

All human kind will someday grow up to be duty bound to something. They will have responsibilities. They will be obligated to carry out those duties and responsibilities. Jesus holds us responsible for growing in the knowledge of Him.

Every branch in me that beareth not fruit he taketh away: and every branch that beareth fruit, he purgeth it, that it may bring forth more fruit.
- John 15:2

As newborn babes, desire the sincere milk of the word, that ye may grow thereby. - 1 Peter 2:2

But grow in grace, and in the knowledge of our Lord and Saviour Jesus Christ. To him be glory both now and forever. Amen. - 2 Peter 3:18

Most 21st century Christians do not believe they are obligated to move past just knowing God. There is a difference in knowing God and really knowing God. Christians have responsibilities. They receive responsibilities from choices and experiences. They are also held responsible for growing in the knowledge of God themselves. Christians must learn to properly handle and manage both sets of responsibilities.

The word burden in the Hebrew is *Phortion* - pronounced Phor-tee-ion. The word simply means load. The English word for *Phortion* is fortune. The word fortune represents a great amount of something. The loads or burdens that people have are faults of their conscience of which they must do things themselves in the way they were trained to resolve the faults.

At the Discipleship Center (DC) where I pastor, I have noticed that most people who seriously desire to live for God are around the age of twenty-five. They learn to handle things in the manner which perhaps their parents taught them or through the suggestions of other people. Because of this, people carry a huge amount of faults and handle them according to their own knowledge. Many are not aware of their faults that are oppressing their very own soul. Because they are not Spirit led, the burdens are too much to handle.

When you are spiritual, you learn the importance of understanding the burden. You want to understand why they are present. You want to understand its purpose. You want to understand how it came into your life. Dwelling on them without thinking how to resolve them will not make you feel any better. This is the typical life of a Christian who claims to have the Holy Spirit in them, but fails to properly utilize what they have.

God did not create humankind to be filled with worries. Your body was not designed to take on the stress of worrying. When Christians are not taught how to benefit fully from having the Holy Spirit, they continue to process issues with the understanding offered through the course of this world.

> *Wherein in time past ye walked according to the course of this world, according to the prince of the power of the air, the spirit that now worketh in the children of disobedience. - Ephesians 2:2*

The course of this world is the root cause of why people are burdened down with issues. The course of this world continues to educate, coach and program people, including unlearned Christians, on how to cope with the burdens they face. First and foremost, you should be asking God to reveal to you the root cause of the burden. List your burdens so you can have an idea as to what you are facing each day. Burdens were never created to be heavy to deal with. They were meant to teach people how to depend on the Holy Spirit's guidance.

> *To everything there is a season, and a time to every purpose under the heaven: A time to be born, and a time to die; a time to plant, and a time to pluck up that which is planted; A time to kill, and a time to heal; a time to break down, and a time to build up; A time to weep, and a time to laugh; a time to mourn, and a time to dance; A time to cast away stones, and a time to gather stones together; a time to embrace, and a time to refrain from embracing; A time to get, and a time to lose; a time to keep, and a time to cast away; A time to rend, and a time to*

> *sew; a time to keep silence, and a time to speak; A time to love, and a time to hate; a time of war, and a time of peace. What profit hath he that worketh in that wherein he laboureth? I have seen the travail which God hath given to the sons of men to be exercised in it. - Ecclesiastes 3:1-10*

We always teach our partners at the Discipleship Center (DC) to prepare themselves each day for some type of exercise, test and spiritual warfare. You never know what is about to hit you at any given moment. Every test that comes our way is not from satan. If they are, it is only because God allows it to be so. It is because God wants you to learn something from the test. It is not for you to avoid or to push aside, and they will not go away until they are dealt with properly. This is the reason why some tests do not appear to get resolved. The test will become burdensome because you chose not to take the time to understand its purpose and learn the lesson. Once you understand its purpose, then the proper action plan has to be implemented by you, the individual.

Knowing how to handle what comes your way is very important. What knocks the Christian in the seat of defeat each time is ignorance of what is transpiring in their life at any given moment. The pastor(s) that God assigns to your life will not be with you every day of the week to nurture you. Nurturing the Word of God in you is your daily responsibility, not the pastor.

When people are burdened with things it is because they lack understanding of things and have not learned to dialogue with the Holy Spirit living inside of them. Overloaded burdens can sometimes open the door for certain spirits to operate in the mind of people such as oppression and depression. If this is you, it is because your spiritual life is not up to par in God.

Personal burdens can keep you away from answers that God wants to give you. Personal burdens can communicate information to your mind that nothing else matters and nothing else is important, even the Word of God.

God gives your pastor(s) answers to what you need to help transform your mind so you can handle burdens properly. This is a process. It does not happen to you automatically. You have to be transformed in your mind to trust the action plans given to you by your pastor(s). There should be consistency in your pastor's messages to transform you from your old ways of doing things into new ways of doing things. Mixed messages without the primary focus on building your relationship with God should be a red flag. Pastors are to be on a track of taking their flock from someone old to someone new and the learner should apply what's being given to them. Christians should not be idle in their faith.

As ye have therefore received Christ Jesus the Lord, so walk ye in him. Rooted and built up in him, and established in the faith as ye have been taught, abounding therein with thanksgiving.
- Colossians 2:6-7

Personal burdens will stop your growth in God. When you have good pastors who know that you should always move from faith to faith, they expect you to take actions to better yourself. It's your responsibility to accept and receive the action plan that they give you as needed. If no follow-up process is in place, the course of this world will pull you back and away from your pastors, the ministry and those whom God has assigned to be a part of your life.

As you are becoming spiritual, everything you do matters. Everything you say matters. How you function throughout the day matters. Every plan or schema you have learned since being brought into this world matters.

You must learn to understand things in order to become spiritual. You must learn how to operate properly in your mind. You live in a natural land, born with a natural mind, which takes spiritual understanding and thinking to not be burdened down with things. Your old and original ways of seeing, hearing and understanding things must cease. The course of this world will challenge you in this area. It wants to maintain control of your thinking without you knowing how much of a load you have.

> *Come unto me, all ye that labour and are heavy laden, and I will give you rest. Take my yoke upon you, and learn of me; for I am meek and lowly in heart: and ye shall find rest unto your souls. For my yoke is easy, and my burden is light.*
> *- Matthew 11:28-30*

There is a more excellent way of living in this life. Jesus said **come to me**, you who are finding yourself working hard just trying to do right; come to me you who are working multiple jobs to survive in this physical land; come to me you who are working hard to keep food on the table and clothes on you and your family's back; come to me you who are working hard in your minds to make what should have been simple decisions end up being hard decisions; come to me you who are working overtime in your minds and it is causing you to be frustrated and tired.

The Holy Spirit's plan, outlines and schemas while living in this world are easy to handle. The burdens that Jesus made reference to represent God's course or ways, paths, provisions, patterns and schemas for people to live by in this world. They are all full of light. The Holy Spirit wants to take you down a road with high visibility using spiritual eyes.

When you begin to dwell in the land of Christ, being the mind of Christ, things are supposed to change in your life. Certain things should not get on your nerves or affect you as they did in times past. You are not supposed to get easily upset or offended about things. You are not supposed to be worrying, panicking, fretting or having strong concerns about things.

Heavy laden again refers to the amount of weight in your life. Personal overloaded burdens cause headaches, sleepless nights with your days completely full so that you do not have time for God. These are all common traits of the course of this world that have taken control over your life. Jesus said if these things describe you, I invite you to come to me in a different way than before and I will give you rest.

Jesus said give me the yokes of bondage that this world have taught you to live by...and then be willing to take what I have to offer you. If you do so ye shall find rest unto your souls. When you accept the plan to give things up just to become spiritual, a tearing away has to happen in your life. Because you are so accustomed to doing things your way, your flesh will not want to let go easily so the Holy Spirit can take control.

> *For the flesh lusteth against the Spirit, and the Spirit against the flesh: and these are contrary the one to the other: so that ye cannot do the things that ye would. - Galatians 5:17*

You will have to fight, and knowing who you are fighting against is VERY important. People are not the reason why the fight is hard. It is spiritual wickedness that is working inside of you that must be dealt with properly. This will require you being a part of a deliverance ministry.

Most 21st century churches don't have a deliverance ministry with people who specialize in casting out evil spirits. The average Christian finds it hard to believe they can have an evil spirit in them while operating with a gift of God in them as well. A deliverance ministry consists of a location that involves a pastor or team such as a five-fold ministry that has personal deliverance skills and their main goal and responsibility is to see people free from demonic oppressions and afflictions. You will struggle trying to become spiritual without a deliverance ministry. Things may appear to be awful while going through deliverance, but it is worth it.

Better is the end of a thing than the beginning thereof: and the patient in spirit is better than the proud in spirit. - Ecclesiastes 7:8

When you decided to really become spiritual, things are supposed to be rough as you are transitioning from what the course of this world has taught you. You can be a Christian and still not be spiritual. Therefore the course of this world has taught you certain patterns and schemas through religion which will not truly make you spiritual.

Your flesh will cause your personal burdens to be much larger to take on than simply taking the time to understand one Scripture in the Bible. Your personal burdens will keep you away from God.

As you embrace becoming spiritual, you will be challenged to change your perception about God in many ways. This is frightening to many who are heavy into religion and not in relationship with God. This is because they have only known to see, hear, and understand things their way for so long.

People who are not open to change or to trying something new are deeply involved in religion. Religion embraces personal burdens and will prevent you from trusting and depending on the Holy Spirit. Relationship with the Lord will change this perception in you. Relationship moves you closer to God. Religion just gives you a surface level understanding of God.

Religion has taught and programmed people to remain comfortable with where they are. Religion will have people dealing with burdens using traditional means. This will consist of them leaning more to their own understanding and not putting on the new wineskins with the Lord. This is where humility plays a major role in you. You have to be humble and be willing to accept new things. This will also require a huge amount of understanding.

Happy is the man that findeth wisdom, and the man that getteth understanding. – Proverbs 13:3

It takes time to become spiritual. Always ask your pastors for understanding of the new things that you are hearing. Ask the Holy Spirit for understanding. You just do not get saved, receive the Holy Spirit and shazam, your entire life of seeing, hearing, doing, and understanding things have been corrected. It takes time, a great amount of humility, willingness to be corrected and understanding with patience.

Your feelings may get hurt as the truth is coming. When this happens, understand this is the flesh responding to your emotions to not accept the truth and to not be willing to let go of the course this world has taught you. If your feelings are hurt, this is a good thing. It is a sign that you have something illegal operating inside of you.

Do not be angry with your pastors nor anyone they may have assigned to work with you. You are not to see them as mere human beings, but agents working for God. This is a critical part of your process of becoming spiritual.

God wants you to understand your burdens and subsequently other people's burdens as well. God wants you to understand and resolve things properly. Things that happen to you were never designed to become a burden to you.

When you have learned to understand and handle things properly, your body will function in its most healthy state. When things become burdensome, they can bring unhealthy conditions to the human body. This is evident when a person has not become truly spiritual. They can be a Christian and still not have learned to handle things with the mind of Christ. God is a Spirit and they that think to handle things in the manner as He does will do so with a spiritual mind.

Chapter 9-Defeating the Spirit of Denial

I be full, and deny thee, and say, Who is the LORD?
or lest I be poor, and steal, and take the name of my
God in vain. - Proverbs 30:9

What is denial? Denial is an assertion that something said, believed or alleged is false. It represents the refusal to believe a doctrine, theory, or the like. It is the disbelief in the existence or reality of a thing. In the business world, it is the refusal to satisfy a claim, request or desire. Denial is simply saying no.

People say no to several things because they give answers from their emotions first. People rarely think or try to understand things before they speak. People have been trained to respond this way generationally. Because of denial playing a major role in the lives of people, they reject all forms of real truth that has the potential to bring deliverance.

The demonic spirit world has taught people to say NO when it is time for truth to enter into their lives. As you are becoming spiritual, it is important that you understand truth is on your side.

And ye shall know the truth, and the truth shall
make you free. - John 8:32

Jesus declared that you will know the truth, or be brought to the point of knowing the truth, and it is this truth that is going to make you free. You need freedom to think. You need freedom to think on the things of God. You need to operate with supernatural freedom in your mind in order to maintain your relationship with the Lord.

> *Jesus saith unto him, I am the way, the truth, and the life: no man cometh unto the Father, but by me.*
> *- John 16:6*

Truth is the true or actual state of a matter. Truth is the opposite of denial. Truth is God's reality. Truth is fact. When you learn to live by being truthful with yourself, you are preparing yourself for freedom to come into your life. Truth changes your environment. Truth gives you personal understanding of yourself and others.

Defeating the spirit of denial is another important factor. Denial can keep you filled with guilt. Denial will always keep you in the dark. Denial can become a major part of a person's life. They become comfortable in the things they do and say. No one can convince them to think differently.

As you are becoming spiritual in God, the spirit of denial can cause you to not become free to serve God. People are faced with decisions everyday whether personal or business. Some of these decisions are simple to make, while others are more difficult.

All people have personal battles.

When one makes the decision to become spiritual, they are faced with the truth about themselves and others they may love.

Becoming spiritual challenges what people have learned and have grown accustomed to. This is truth coming up against denial.

Satan hates the truth because it is designed to set people free from years of bondage whether physical, natural, physiological, psychological, emotional or spiritual. When truth is present, understanding of things should come along with it. People go into denial because of a lack of understanding.

> *They profess that they know God; but in works they deny him, being abominable, and disobedient, and unto every good work reprobate. - Titus 1:16*

When truth comes knocking at your door, you have to accept these things as being true about yourself. You cannot be abominable. The word abominable means to become unpleasant or disagreeable towards things.

Becoming spiritual requires being tutored by spiritual leaders who are already spiritually mature or stable. As they give directions and guidance it is important that you are obedient to their instructions.

There is a danger in not obeying the instructions from servants of God. People who operate in a spirit of disobedience can develop a reprobate mind. To have a reprobate mind is to be given over to doing things their way instead of God's way. Christians can operate with a reprobate mind and not even know it. Their works can be good in the eyes of men, but from God's eyes, He finds no value in what they do.

Lengthy denial leads to reprobate lifestyles. To consistently deny you have problems means you have placed yourself on the same level as Jesus Christ, who is without sin and knows all things. Is this really you?

In the world today, we have people who communicate in what I call "cell type relationships". We have the rich living in certain parts of our cities, and we have the poor living in other parts. Depending upon the status they are living in, people consult with individuals that can offer the best solution for the problem they are dealing with.

Places of worship are usually the last place people come to when looking for a way out. This is because of a lack of proper pastoral teaching. God has made it known that when a person has heard about the life changing power of Jesus Christ and makes the decision to live by the ways of the Lord, and to not deny it, they will find favor with the Lord.

Good understanding giveth favour: but the way of transgressors is hard. - Proverbs 13:15

Good understanding can only be received by making a commitment to want to understand the Word of God. God gives us pastors according to Jeremiah 3:15 according to His own heart to feed people with proper understanding. As you trust in pastors who have the heart of God, you will find favor in terms of growing in the knowledge of God, being filled with the Spirit of God in all wisdom, knowledge, and understanding, and in all manner of workmanship which details all that you do. People who deny that God is not guiding pastors with the heart of God will face difficulties becoming spiritual.

If you do not have a good understanding of something, you will automatically reject anything new. Religious people will deny God is with people and they will reject anything new about God.

As you are maturing spiritually, you will fight an internal fight to gain proper understanding. If you deny the truth as it comes, your life will continue to be hard. Nothing will come easy and there will always be a constant struggle to get ahead.

A transgressor is a person in denial who constantly kicks against the things of God. They will refute correction and direction, and murmur and complain against leadership because of what they have been programmed to know and understand about themselves, other people and especially the church body.

A transgressor cannot be trusted; they are unreliable; they are insecure, and in some cases, they are dangerous to be around. When a person who does not have a relationship with the Lord and is faced with a tough decision, they are typically found in one of these categories.

Another sign that someone is battling the spirit of denial is when they refuse to accept apostolic order, judgment, establishment, government, and authority. When the first sin was committed, that marked the first occasion of man having to give an account for doing wrong. As a result of this act, the spirit of denial became alive in the world.

> *And the man said, The woman whom thou gavest to be with me, she gave me of the tree, and I did eat.*
> *- Genesis 3:12*

The first man denied doing something wrong and put the blame on the woman according to Genesis 3:9-12. Because of the fall of man, people continue to deny things daily. This is often seen as one having accusations towards others to not accept the responsibility themselves.

> *My spirit shall not always strive with man, for that he also is flesh. - Genesis 6:3*

As long as we are in this flesh, we are going to have to deal with this spirit of denial that will try to overtake us and over power the judgment and direction of the Holy Spirit living in us. You must not allow the flesh to win this battle. Doing so will cause you to struggle while in your process of maturing spiritually.

As a people, we must be careful not to let people who walk in darkness, which also represents those operating in the state of denial, to deter you from maturing spiritually. They can cause you to doubt the power of God who works life changing wonders in your life. Trials are forever changing therefore people's perspectives are changing.

Life will keep you so busy working with other things that you will not have time for personal spiritual development. This is a warning sign that you must learn to identify in yourself. Before the fall, both the man and the woman had a spiritual connection with God. God's original plan was for people to remain spiritual in Him. Because of one man's act of disobedience, it made it difficult for people to find that spiritual connection with God, mainly because people who knew God were not willing to live right and teach others how to connect with God as well.

Many people live and die never understanding why they simply could not stop doing wrong. My attempt in writing this book is to cause one to understand who we are really fighting against, and one of the main opponents in this world is the spirit of denial. The devil does not want people to know the primary reason for Christ coming into the world was to take away the sins of the world which causes humans to just simply do things that are wrong.

People do wrong naturally, which is the result of our fallen nature that occurred in the Garden of Eden. This gave demonic spirits access to our minds. Demons and evil spirits cause people to do wrong through the works of darkness. This is the unseen activity that is undetected by the human eye. The natural eye will reject this fact.

The spirit of denial operates in darkness. The spirit of denial will convince people that demons and evil spirits cannot exist in people, especially Christians. The spirit of denial will cause them to believe their ways of living are not dirty or polluted.

> *Wherewithal shall a young man cleanse his way?*
> *By taking heed thereto according to thy word.*
> *- Psalm 119:9*

When we allow our sinful ways to take advantage of us, even after hearing that God wants to help us, we bring additional problems on ourselves and then our faith really has to kick in to believe God for a way out.

You will not become spiritual doing things your way. Paul does a magnificent job defining what people want to do by giving his own personal testimony and even admitting that he himself has to struggle with things in his mind, and things on the inside of him that continued to cause him to contradict what was right to do. To operate with the mind of Christ, you cannot deny the wrong that is currently in your mind. You cannot deny the wrong things that are within you. When you are in the right spiritual atmosphere, these things will reveal itself.

When you are making progress in your personal relationship with God, these things will manifest in you. You have to be ready to accept them in order for change to come.

> *For I know that in me dwelleth no good thing: for to will is present with me; but how to perform that which is good I find not. For the good that I would I do not: but the evil which I would not, that I do. Now if I do that I would not, it is no more I that do it, but sin that dwelleth in me. I find then a law, that, when I would do good, evil is present with me. For I delight in the law of God after the inward man. But I see another law in my members, warring against the law of my mind, and bringing me into captivity to the law of sin which is in my members.*
> *- Romans 7:18-23*

It was through Paul's testimony that I have a much better understanding of why the saints of God, and people in general, continue to rebel or stay in opposition to God and people. They never realize this nor do they begin to think to ponder why. Paul describes his flesh as *his sinful nature*. He acknowledges that something bad is in him. He describes the condition that he desires to do what is good at times and continues to carry out the bad instead. Nobody is forcing or convincing Paul to do wrong because it is in his nature. It is another law that will work in us if we do not learn to put it to death through the power of the Holy Spirit.

You cannot deny this other law working in you if you want to become spiritual. Before the fall of man, Adam's mind did not require a law or knowledge to choose between good and evil, right or wrong. After the fall, men and women began to struggle in life, struggling with decisions, under the influence of denial, not understanding that God sent his Son to die for our sins, to help us in this area.

Our inward man, which consists of the mind, the soul, the lower nature, our human spirit and our body, wants to be in a position of learning how to delight in the law or ways of God. This connection is made possible by the Holy Spirit.

According to Wikipedia.com, our mind consists of our consciousness, perception, thinking and judgment. Our soul consists of the immortal essence of a person. The human spirit consists of our intellect, emotions, fears, passions, and creativity. The lower nature makes reference to the place where negative qualities seen in man are derived from. Demonic forces want control of our lower nature. This is the reason why there is such a fight internally.

To become spiritual in God, you cannot deny the fact that the internal fight is a spiritual battle that can only be won by using spiritual weapons. The only way that people are going to be able to live a better life, they must understand the reason why they are in darkness, or in the dark of things, where no light has illuminated or turned on in their minds to show them a more excellent way of life. They must move away from this state of denial, and learn how to be led by the Spirit. It's a constant fight that we have, but we have help if we truly have Christ in us. Learn to associate with the right people who understand how to operate from a spiritual perspective and you will then experience freedom from denial.

Chapter 10-Defeating the Spirit of Fear

For God hath not given us the spirit of fear; but of power, and of love, and of a sound mind. - 2 Timothy 1:7

What is fear and where did it come from? First and foremost, you need to know that fear did not come from God. Notice how the spirit of fear is associated with the mind in this Scripture. To have a sound mind means to have a mind that is free from injury, damage, defect and disease, and that is in good condition, very secure and very reliable. This gives you an idea of one having the mind of Christ.

Fear contaminates the mind and opens the door for the mind to become injured, damaged, and full of defects and disease. Fear puts the mind in bad condition. People who constantly operate in fear are very insecure and they are very unreliable. They are often ashamed of themselves and they have a fear of being embarrassed.

There is no fear in love; but perfect love casteth out fear: because fear hath torment. - 1 John 4:18

Fear has a voice. Fear can talk to you on a consistent basis without a person even noticing it. Fear will tell you to not trust in certain people. Fear told Adam in his mind, God is upset with you, you are exposed and you no longer have a spiritual covering over you. Fear told Adam to do something he had never done before. Fear said,

"Adam, you are now exposed, hide yourself from the presence of God." Before this took place, Adam had no reason to hide from God. The spirit of fear can run the lives of people and torment them without any notice.

Torment has to do with correction and punishment. When someone, not just one time, continues to correct and punish you, you are being tormented. When fear is operating in the mind of people, fear can give them counsel to believe known good things are bad and known bad things are good. People suffer in their thinking because of fear.

People who continue to reject solid biblical teachings don't know if they are being tormented in their mind by the spirit of fear. Fear tells them on a consistent basis this style of teaching is wrong. Fear tells them to stay away from strategic decrees and do not read any strategic declarations given by the Holy Spirit. Decrees and declarations are simply bold statements spoken into existence by the Christian believer.

1 John 4:18 goes on to say *He that feareth is not made perfect in love.* Becoming spiritual is being made perfected in the nature of God. How will people become prophetic people if they fear what others may say about them by choosing to be apostolic? How will people become apostolic people when listening to fear telling them in their mind to keep rejecting apostolic order? Fear will tell them you can still become someone new, just do not listen to apostolic people. This is a lie from the devil.

As I was in my process of becoming spiritual, a lot of things began to change in my life. I had to learn to accept the knowledge of the truth after coming into the understanding of it. Your relationship with God will change as you are becoming spiritual. You cannot become fearful of this change, but instead you must accept this change.

The spirit of fear will attempt to convince you to not accept this change easily. You will question just about everything you do or say. This is seasonal and you are to expect this kind of result. The aim is to educate you with spiritual knowledge so you can operate in the power of God, full of God's love so you can avoid making the mistakes of judging people, and for you to simply have a stable mind. An unstable mind is a double minded person. The spirit of fear will grow off of a double minded person.

My aim in writing this book is two-fold. The first is to cause you as kingdom builders to step out of your comfort zone and for you to no longer operate in fear as you are making progress in spiritual growth. Secondly, the Lord wants you to no longer procrastinate in general with regards to how you are to live and to allow situations and circumstances to take place in your lives on a day-to-day basis. God is still speaking to Christians every day.

God has been saying, "You have the Holy Spirit in you, and you have what it takes to get the job done." Many Christians are unable to see this for themselves. God knows us better than we know ourselves. We tend to look at ourselves and judge ourselves unworthy because of the deeds done in our bodies even with the Holy Spirit abiding in us. Therefore we make little, if not any, attempt to align ourselves properly with the Holy Spirit. This is a major issue that many Christians need deliverance from. God can say you are mighty, yet your situations and circumstances can cause you to say and to believe you are not.

> *And such were some of you: but ye are washed, but ye are sanctified, but ye are justified in the name of*

the Lord Jesus, and by the Spirit of our God. - 1 Corinthians 6:11

God does not see our past faults like we see them. God is ready to use us. The spirit of fear will convince you that you are not approved to do a work for God. In becoming spiritual, you must learn to not allow this to happen.

The Word of God says you are sanctified. The word sanctified means to be set apart or to be changed. Changed in how you think, how you understand and in what you do. After much deliverance you will respond differently to things. It is the process that people must go through that blocks this from happening. People will drag their feet in terms of implementing actions. They may not feel fear telling them not to do it, but their actions will clearly show the spirit of fear in operation.

The word justified here means to be made free. This is a part of deliverance, which takes time. The length of time varies with each individual and there are a number of factors involved in the process. One thing I have noticed at the Discipleship Center (DC) is people who have not been churched as much can more easily accept being told they may have evil spirits working in them and controlling their thoughts at will. For people who have been churched for many years, I've noticed how quickly they would reject this statement. We noticed the un-churched are quick to assist others in deliverance while the churched are very fearful during this time although Jesus said these were clear indications of the power of God working in them that believe.

And these signs shall follow them that believe; In my name shall they cast out devils; they shall speak with new tongues; - Mark 16:17

Jesus clearly said *And these signs shall follow <u>them</u> that believe.* Are you a believer of Jesus Christ? Do you believe you have the power of God in you to cast out devils in Jesus name? Do you think God put a limit of how many believers can cast out devils in Jesus name? It doesn't matter if you have a title of a pastor, elder, evangelist or not, simply if you have received Jesus Christ and understand the power of having the Holy Spirit working in you through a personal relationship with God, you have the power to cast out devils in Jesus name without fear.

> *And, behold, there was a woman which had a spirit of infirmity eighteen years, and was bowed together, and could in no wise lift up herself...And ought not this woman, being a daughter of Abraham, whom satan hath bound, lo, these eighteen years, be loosed from this bond on the Sabbath day? - Luke 13:11, 16*

In the Scriptures above, Jesus was reasoning with the Jews in hopes of them understanding the need of seeing people afflicted by certain spirits and a desire to see them free. Here is a woman who was in a restricted position for eighteen years because of a spirit of infirmity and no one seemed to care about her condition. People should have the heart of Christ to indentify such conditions and desire to see them free. Fear will tell a person that's just the way they are and they will always be this way. Jesus desired freedom and deliverance for this woman. He had the authority in Him to bring healing and to set her free. He was setting an example for believers to desire the same freedom and deliverance for people bound by various types of infirmities.

Spiritual people have the authority in Jesus Christ to bring healing, freedom and deliverance to others. Fear will say you don't have the faith to heal this person. This can occur when you don't understand the authority given to you by Jesus Christ. Fear will block you from fully understanding this authority.

Fear will cause you to reject the thought and doubt in your heart that it can be done. People must understand the power of fear and what it does in the mind.

In the previous chapters we learned how sin entered into the world by one man. Included in this was the ability to do wrong in all aspects of life. When the first sin was committed, that marked the first account by man having to give an account for doing wrong, and as a result, the spirit of denial became alive in the world because the man denied that he was wrong and put the blame on the woman.

> *And the man said, The woman whom thou gavest to be with me, she gave me of the tree, and I did eat.*
> *- Genesis 3:12*

If we were to back up some verses, we will find that in addition to the spirit of denial coming into the world, the Bible lets us know that the spirit of fear also came into the world. When God went looking for the man, the man and his wife hid themselves when they heard the voice of God walking in the garden.

> *And they heard the voice of the Lord God walking in the garden in the cool of the day: and Adam and his wife hid themselves from the presence of the Lord God amongst the trees of the garden. And the Lord God called unto Adam, and said unto him,*

> *Where art thou? And he said, I heard thy voice in the garden, and I was afraid, and he gave the reason why because I was naked; and I hid myself.*
> *- Genesis 3:8-10*

Today we still see men and women who are called of God still fighting against and hiding from their full potential because of this spirit of fear.

Fear causes people to hide because of the decisions and mistakes they have made in times past. Jesus on many occasions spoke to different people telling them and us as well, to "fear not" concerning the things that we see, have questioned, have done and of the things that God is calling us to do. The spirit of fear caused Joseph to go back and forth wondering in his mind - should he or should he not take Mary to be his wife?

> *Behold, the angel of the Lord appeared unto him in a dream, saying, Joseph, thou son of David, fear not to take unto thee Mary thy wife: for that which is conceived in her is of the Holy Ghost.*
> *- Matthew 1:20*

Not long after this, Jesus entered into a ship, his disciples followed him on the ship and while on the ship, a strong storm suddenly came and frightened them.

> *And when he was entered into a ship, his disciples followed him. And, behold, there arose a great tempest in the sea, insomuch that the ship was covered with the waves: but he was asleep. And his disciples came to him, and awoke him, saying, Lord, save us: we perish. And he saith unto them, Why are*

ye fearful, O ye of little faith? Then he arose, and rebuked the winds and the sea; and there was a great calm. - Matthew 8:23-26

The spirit of fear in the land has kept millions of Christians from coming into their full potential. Fear has taught them to be afraid of change, being different, thinking outside of the box, moving away from operating in religion or having a relationship with God.

When trouble comes, people that have a spirit of religion are programmed to handle the situation using approaches and principals that may not be totally biblical. They mostly rely on their own and other people's ideologies and philosophies that come from years of religion. They may not be transformed from a worldly mind.

People who have a relationship with the Lord however are relationship driven. They want to know how things work and what to do to resolve matters. They are not afraid of trying something different or something new. They embrace change to understand God better. They don't mind praying different kind of prayers. I call them strategic prayers that are designed to pin point and dismantle specific spirits from afflicting them.

As a result of fear, religious Christians will not venture down the path of learning something new and understanding their real enemies. Christians that have a relationship with God learn to love and embrace this. Relationship driven Christians truly take on the mind of Christ. They learn to stay calm in certain situations. They exemplify meekness through the guidance of the Holy Spirit. Meekness is simply having a humbled spirit. They are taught how not to panic when the heat is on.

Be sober, be vigilant; because your adversary the devil, as a roaring lion, walketh about, seeking whom he may devour. - 1 Peter 5:8

To be sober in this case has to do with staying cool, calm and collected concerning life many events. Their blood pressure nor stress levels go up because they have become educated about the events that take place from day to day. To be vigilant is to have the ability to maintain attention and alertness over a prolonged period of time. Believers with a strong relationship will remain aware of what is going on at all times.

They are not always sleeping, but watching as well as praying about things. They learn to understand the enemy's plan of attack, schemas, layouts and agendas. They pray strategic prayers against the enemy's plan that are effective. Many Christians who are very religious are unaware of these things. The enemy sees them as no threat against his mission.

When a born again believer moves into relationship through the process of growing spiritually, the enemy ramps up their plan to devour or put to death spiritual growth in them that could put them out of business. The main reason is because that Christian has made the decision to become educated about spiritual warfare and they are ready to develop a relationship with the Lord.

When you are learning how to become spiritual, you should always be mindful again of who is operating in people. You must not be afraid of investigating and learning their patterns of communicating and giving advice. Your main objective is to grow in all wisdom and understanding of the Scripture.

If you are married and your spouse is a Christian also, they should have the same goal. If there are things that negate these actions, do not be afraid, but suspect that it is the working of the enemy.

While we are in our maturation stage, we too have to be mindful of the personal tasks that we have. God is teaching us how to become spiritual in Him. In this, the Lord is giving us tasks to perform, things to say, things to not do, and things to not say. We cannot be afraid or assume that the outcome is not going to come out right. We cannot be afraid of thinking we may make a mistake in the things that God has given us to do! We have got to trust and believe in our God and the power that He has given us.

> *But beware of men: for they will deliver you up to the councils, and they will scourge you in their synagogues; And ye shall be brought before governors and kings for my sake, for a testimony against them and the Gentiles. - Matthew 10:17-18*

There are cases where people will bring judgment upon you because of the change you have made. They will make an example of you saying they were right and you were wrong. They will attempt anything to cause your mind to shift back into a religious mindset instead of a relational mindset. Religious mindsets are fixed mindsets. They do not want to change and will try to prevent you from changing if you let them. Relationship mindsets are growth mindsets. Again they are open for change for the betterment of themselves and for their families.

The spirit of fear will also cause people that are not a part of the kingdom of God to operate in the same manner. They may not like you, just because…and for fear that you may receive something before they do, they will try to bring you down...but do not you worry...Jesus said this many times:

> *Fear them not therefore: for there is nothing covered, that shall not be revealed; and hid, that shall not be known. - Matthew 10:26*

> *And fear not them which kill the body, but are not able to kill the soul: but rather fear him which is able to destroy both soul and body in hell. - Matthew 10:28*

> *Fear ye not therefore, ye are of more value than many sparrows. - Matthew 10:31*

In order to become spiritual, you must acknowledge the possibility of the spirit of fear operating in you and learn to renounce and denounce it each time it attempts to come back.

> *Proclaim ye this among the Gentiles; Prepare war, wake up the mighty men, let all the men of war draw near; let them come up: Beat your plowshares into swords, and your pruning hooks into spears: let the weak say, I am strong. - Joel 3:9-10*

Having fear will cause you to become weak in many areas of your life. You can quote Scriptures, but in the enemy's eyes you are not mighty. Demons know when people are operating in fear. Medically, the person's frontal cortex shrinks at signs of fear. You should decree that never again will you say you are weak concerning any matter, but instead to say you are strong.

Educated Christians become mighty Christians. Uneducated Christians remain weak Christians. If you have ever said you are weak in any area of life, the phrase comes from the spirit of fear.

When God comes into your life, you begin to be powerful and strong. You are moving beyond that timid person. You are becoming that strong person. You must know and believe you are strong in every aspect of your life. You must know and believe you are strong in thought, understanding, knowledge, imagination and emotionally, nothing wavering. There are spiritual tools to be used in defeating the spirit of fear and all underlying spirits with the potential to operate in people.

For those serious Christians who are ready to move from religion into relationship with the Lord, your first move should be to locate a deliverance ministry. This type of ministry is imperative when shifting from one style of life to another.

With the Holy Spirit living in us and His word maturing us, we have no need to be afraid when God gives us something to do. Why? Because His word gives us the power and the strength to decree, to declare, and to establish change in ourselves, our families, and in the lives of God's people.

The more I think about this, the more I think of others in the kingdom of God who are gifted to do great things for the Lord. God has spoken to them about doing kingdom work, but the spirit of fear has taken a toll on their mind because of what they have been told by tares in operation. Timothy was being challenged to reach out to true Christians who were being misled by evil spirits operating in their lives.

In many ministries, they have taught leaders how to get people to follow their doctrine or agenda based on lies the enemy has sowed in their minds. These are just some of the important facts that every Christian should know, understand and accept.

Can you accept these things to be true?

If you are struggling to accept the statements made in this book, there is a good possibility that you are battling against the enemy called satan in your mind who desires to keep you in spiritual darkness. Becoming spiritual is the way out. God intended it to be this way. Yes and Amen!

Calvin B. Collins, Sr.

Chapter 11-Being Made Aware of the Times

And the LORD came, and stood, and called as at other times, Samuel, Samuel. Then Samuel answered, Speak; for thy servant heareth.
- 1 Samuel 3:10

In the previous chapter, the Lord revealed to us one of the leading causes why people continue to live difficult lives as a result of one act of sin. This sin was an act of disobedience. It was this act that introduced pride into the world and birthed a spirit into the world called denial. We learned that people who are full of pride are always in denial. People in denial do wrong to themselves and others.

Notice in the above passage of Scripture how the Lord continued to call Samuel's name. Samuel was not in the greatest position to hear God speaking to him at certain times of his life. People can find themselves in this same pattern of not hearing God due to life's experiences. In this chapter, you will see how sin, which simply describes wrongful ways of living, if left unchecked can cause people to operate improperly in the kingdom of God.

As you are growing in the knowledge of God, it is important that you are aware of who the real workers are in the world of God's ministries or churches. You need to know that there are some people in the church world that appear to be doing well, but they do not love God's people in the way they should.

What most Christians do not understand is that when God puts people together, He is forming a team to do ministry work. This work consists of deliverance for the team first and then deliverance for those that God sends to the ministry. You have to be delivered from things first before you can bring deliverance to someone else.

> *And the Lord said, Simon, Simon, behold, Satan hath desired to have you, that he may sift you as wheat: But I have prayed for thee, that thy faith fail not: and when thou art converted, strengthen thy brethren. - Luke 22:31-32*

In this Scripture, the enemy satan desired to have control of Peter called Simon's mind. Satan desired to sift him as wheat. In sifting wheat, there are other parts of the wheat that appear to be wheat but it is not wheat. It is actually called chaff. Chaff looks very similar to wheat.

In Peter's case, instead of the Word of God remaining pure in his mind, satan wants to keep the impure stuff in his mind while causing Peter to think he is right at times, when he could possibly be thinking wrong. Satan desires for God's people to think this way. This is his preferred way as he attempts to block spiritual growth in people. Satan knows that if he can keep confusion in the minds of people, they will give up trying to do what is right. Satan wants to keep confusion in their minds so they are not as effective in doing the works of God. When you are becoming spiritual, you should be asking all kinds of questions for clarity sake.

> *Wisdom is the principal thing; therefore get wisdom: and with all thy getting get understanding. - Proverbs 4:7*

The word "principal" in this Scripture means first. People should learn to become wise at what they do first. They should remember the results of things that happen to them in the past so not to repeat the same mistakes again.

Wisdom is understanding. People must desire to have an understanding of things in their minds. People should not come to Jesus Christ blindly without having an understanding of why they should be saved. There are more things about salvation that people must know first, to include a commitment that must be made to a lifestyle to live by. The basics are for your sins to be forgiven and you to receive a ticket that keeps your soul from eternal fire.

As you are becoming spiritual, keep in mind the enemy desires to keep confusion in your mind. You must fight to not allow this to happen. I pray you understand the importance of this.

> *Getting saved will not stop the hell that people live in, it just saves us from going to hell. When you are born again there has to be growth. Without a new mind you will just have salvation.*
> *- Dennis R. Jacobs*

As quoted above, when you are born again, there has to be growth. I say often to our partners at the Discipleship Center (DC), it was never God's will for people to come to know Jesus Christ and be faithful to the ministry only to stay at the same level of growth for many years. God expects us to become well educated in the things of God so that we can do real Kingdom work.

One of the Christian's main objective is for them to get free themselves and then assist in setting others free. The load of ministry work was never meant to fall into the hands of one person, however, this has been the model for many charismatic, evangelical and Pentecostal churches for many years now. Everyone has some type of spiritual gifting in them that is designed to be used in the Kingdom.

In the traditional church today, we have choir members, deacons, ministerial, administrative staff and financial supporters of the ministry who rarely think about understanding kingdom expansion God wants to use people to help lead others out of bondage. If this does not happen, the one or two pastors in charge of hundreds of people will burn out. Everyone owns a piece of the commission to spread the gospel and to bring light to people who are in darkness.

> *For first of all, when ye come together in the church, I hear that there be divisions among you; and I partly believe it. - 1 Corinthians 11:18*

If you are a part of a ministry that has divisions in the body, you need to know and understand that you are not in a spiritually driven ministry. There should not be any divisions going on within the body. All should have understanding and all should be on one accord. If there are splits in the body such as people who are real for God and people who are not and the leaders tolerate the behavior, this is one of the causes why the people cannot receive true deliverance. The local church body will continue to suffer and as new people come in, thus deliverance is hindered.

Spirit led people learn to understand the purpose for ministry. They quickly learn to change certain behaviors in their lives so the proper or prophetic flow can work in the body. If every church member or partner fails to understand their purpose for kingdom living, there will always be division within that local assembly.

These are the times that we live in where people do not want to join together to do a work for the Lord. Again, the reason why is because those people lack deliverance.

When people receive true salvation, what comes with that is deliverance and safety. Becoming Spiritual brings deliverance and safety. You become wiser in the things that you do. Your knowledge increases, which places your life in safer conditions.

He came unto his own, and his own received him not. - John 1:11

When Jesus began his ministry in the world, He came to His own country, and His own people, who were Jews, judged His works and received Him not. They judged Him this way because they were looking at Jesus through natural eyes. Apostles, prophets, pastors, teachers and evangelists that are operating in the apostolic (apo-stolic) and the prophetic are viewed this way today. This is because of the strength of the spirit of denial that is in the land.

Being connected to the right spiritual people is very important as you are growing spiritually. They will help you to understand things better. I am an advocate for edifying ourselves and others. I say all the time if it is not good mail coming into my house then it is considered to be junk mail and I do not want it.

When the true Word of God comes, a spiritual person in God can easily identify it and receive it. They look for words that will build them up and for things that will prepare them for greater things in God. They also learn to identify if the Word will benefit their other brothers and sisters in the Lord.

The reason why Jesus' own people did not receive Him was because they too were under the control of the spirit of denial. These Jews were in denial, and did not believe that Jesus Christ was the Messiah to come. These Jews became corrupt in their thinking and understanding. One example of how leaders can become corrupt in the body of Christ is by allowing themselves to be used by the devil and they in most cases are not aware of it.

> *And after the sop which was called the Last Supper, Satan entered into him being Judas Iscariot. Then said Jesus unto him, That thou doest, do quickly.*
> *- John 13:27*

I often use the above passage of Scripture to prove a point to Christians that satan can reside in the human body. We live in times now of which many Christians do not believe this is possible. This Scripture proves my theory to be correct.

I believe it is possible for Christians to have demons in them. I believe bad spirits are housed in a different location within the body. It is my belief that the Holy Spirit connects to our human spirit and demon spirits can hover over our soul and satan works in this lower nature. For example, if you were to take a glass and place it over a small ball, this gives you an idea of how demons can hover over the soul of man. It is from this area of which the mind of a person is affected with demonic directions and guidance to come against the things of God.

Judas immediately went to work in pursuit of betraying our Lord. When satan was done using this disciple, Judas realized he had shed innocent blood and committed suicide. Who was Jesus talking to in this Scripture when He said "*That thou doest, do quickly*"? Was it Judas or was it satan?

You are correct to say satan. He was not speaking to Judas at the time because satan had already entered into Judas and had taken control of his mind. Now you have another spirit that has entered into Judas' body controlling him and using his voice, eyes, ears, walking just like him, etcetera.

Submitting to the Holy Ghost and becoming spiritual, you will have to believe that bad or evil spirits can enter into the bodies of people and cause them to say and to do things against you as well as others. When you understand this, you will learn to understand yourself and how to properly handle relationships with other people in general.

> *For we wrestle not against flesh and blood, but against principalities, against powers, against the rulers of the darkness of this world, against spiritual wickedness in high places.*
> *- Ephesians 6:12*

We covered the above Scripture in chapter six and made it clear that our real enemy is not with humans which represent flesh and blood, but against principalities, powers, rulers of the darkness of this world and spiritual wickedness in high places. With this understanding, you will discover what makes you do and say certain things. You will discover what blocks you from spiritual growth. You will understand why people do the things they do and say the things they say. You will understand in many cases, it is not the human being who is doing the bad things to people, it is something spiritual that has taken over them.

Being a part of a deliverance ministry will teach you these things and how to break free from them. Satan can be kicked out of people and satan can be prevented from entering in again.

Judas realized he was not guarding his human spirit properly. He repented, gave back the money that was given to him for turning in our Lord, and the Bible recorded that he went and committed suicide by hanging himself.

Your human spirit is connected to the Holy Spirit. When the Holy Spirit is no longer feeding into the human spirit because of what is going on in the lower nature of man, the end result is guilt, condemnation and shame. These three can lead to both spiritual and even physical death.

If you are not focused clearly on what God has called you into then the things God has prepared for you to do can die prematurely. This could consist of many things from personal to spiritual destinations and assignments. In this, we see how the devil can easily enter into the heart of people to cause them to do things, and in many cases, they do not even know that they are operating under demonic influence until it is too late. In becoming spiritual, you must learn to not be quick in judging yourself and people for the wrong that they do without first understanding that they could be under some type of demonic influence.

> *Then said Jesus, Father, forgive them; for they know not what they do. And they parted his raiment, and cast lots. - Luke 23:34*

Jesus gave the perfect action plan for us to use in situations such as this.

As a Christian, we are to love and understand people and know at times that it is not always actual person doing the wrong that they do. If all Christians are taught to understand this, the body of Christ would be much stronger.

Families are weakened because they continue to point the finger at the person instead of the evil spirit. Deliverance is not present therefore the evil spirit is not dealt with. Denial will prevent them from understanding this and so families and lives are torn apart and separation is present in the home and in the church world. Because not all people will believe this, we now have various divisions, although all have and use the same Bible. Because we understand the root cause as to why we ourselves and other people do the things they do, we can say what Jesus said which is "Father forgive them, for they know not what they are doing!"

> *And the God of peace shall bruise Satan under your feet shortly. The grace of our Lord Jesus Christ be with you. Amen. - Romans 16:20*

Paul speaks prophetically unto the Jews decreeing and declaring unto them, that the God of peace shall bruise satan under their feet, shortly!

In other words, Paul was saying that our warfare within the body of Christ will soon be over. We are in those times now. God is speaking. Are we listening and are we doing what we are being asked to do by God through godly leaders and from the spirit of God as well?

The time will come when God will begin to dismantle those leaders who opt to be under the control of demonic spirits, who are operating under the influence of satan, having established themselves within the kingdom of God, taking advantage of God's people using good words and fair speeches. These leaders do this out of a spirit of pride, spirit of ambition, and through unique charismatic ways which causes separation between Christian men and women.

Study the Moabites to learn more on separating spirits. They are determined to dispute things. They give strong criticism or disapproval of things. They have evil conclusions of things without evidence. Study the spirit of Korah to learn more about this spirit.

Christians will find it difficult and challenging in becoming spiritual when various spirits are operating in full force over them. Learn to identify the bad, get delivered and watch yourself grow in the knowledge of God. Bottom line, Jesus is saying that there will come a separation between the two. The enemy will leave you and stay out of you once you have become educated with the truth of God's Word under a renewed mind. We must remember, that it is not our job to say who is going to heaven and who is going to hell. Only God determines that.

In God's view, a child is not just a child; nor is a brother just a brother or an elderly couple just an elderly couple. God has work for all of us to do outside of the four walls of the places of worship, but because of evil spirits operating in leaders within the kingdom, they have taken control and advantage of the innocent for their own personal gain. I have said many times before that it is the job of the pastor to properly educate the people of God with knowledge and understanding about their God given purpose. Pastors must educate Christians in their role within the kingdom of God. Pastors have a responsibility to educate and all of God's people have a responsibility to become educated.

My aim is to help you to become spiritual so that you can become aware of the times that you live in. Real relationship with God can begin with you being in control over your life under God's hand.

About The Author

Pastor Collins has lived in the greater Raleigh, North Carolina area for 25 years, having relocated from his hometown of Memphis, Tennessee in 1989. Upon arrival to Raleigh, he attended a week night church service, heard the Word of God preached and received the salvation of Jesus Christ. In 1995, the Lord called Calvin into the ministry with a request to preach the Word of God. His desire to win lost souls grew to make him a greater witness for God in the communities of Raleigh and surrounding areas. Pastor Collins purchased a public announcement (PA) system and with the leading of the Lord, brought the "Gospel of Christ" more effectively to the streets of Raleigh. On the first night of service, over 30 souls gave their hearts to Jesus Christ and they became Christians. As the gospel was preached, the people witnessed firsthand the power of God changing lives in the communities. As time progressed, there was a great need for continual teaching to show people how to grow and live for God. The name Community Healing and Restoration Ministries, Inc. was established for this work and was granted 501 3c nonprofit status. On August 3, 2008, Pastor Collins officially launched and established the ministry in Zebulon, North Carolina. In 2011 the name was changed to Healing and Restoration Discipleship Center, Inc., otherwise known as "The DC".

Pastor Collins provides strategic, spiritual protocol, transformational, apostolic, prophetic, progressive, and deliverance teachings to Christians who have been wounded in the faith, and to those who are looking for spiritual restoration and training. Pastor Collins stands tall in the five-fold ministry and is a mover and a shaker in the Kingdom of God. Pastor Collins currently resides in Knightdale, North Carolina with his lovely wife Kimberly and is the proud father of three children, his son Calvin B. Collins, Jr., and his twin daughters Karia (Car-rie-ah) and Karington (Care-ring-ton).

About Kingdom Journey Press

Kingdom Journey Press, Inc. is a full-service publishing company specializing in providing customized services to support our clients from the conception of an idea to getting HIStory to the masses! Since the time of inception and in conjunction with our umbrella organization, Kingdom Journey Enterprises, we have become recognized globally for our ability to establish a unique presence, while building relationships with partners and clients consisting of current and aspiring writers, and ministry, business, and community organizations.

Our services include:

- Manuscript Evaluation
- Coaching for current and aspiring authors
- Editing
- Cover and Print Layout Design
- Print and E-Book Format
- Copyright and Distribution
- Marketing and Sales Support

For more information, visit our website at www.kjpressinc.com.

Calvin B. Collins, Sr.

www.ingramcontent.com/pod-product-compliance
Lightning Source LLC
LaVergne TN
LVHW041624070426
835507LV00008B/436